PHARMAPLASIA™

phar•ma•pla•sia (fahr-muh-pley-zhuh) *n.* Rapid, uncontrolled growth in a pharmaceutical company that exceeds its capacity to be managed effectively, resulting in a series of unintended consequences.

PHARMAPLASIA™

phar•ma•pla•sia (fahr-muh-pley-zhuh) *n.* Rapid, uncontrolled growth in a pharmaceutical company that exceeds its capacity to be managed effectively, resulting in a series of unintended consequences.

Michael G. Wokasch

WOKASCH
CONSULTING LLC

Library of Congress Control Number: 2010924833
ISBN: 978-0-9844463-5-1 (hardcover)
ISBN: 978-0-9844463-0-8 (softcover)

Table of Contents

Preface

For some people, time away from everyday activities helps focus the mind on a challenging problem or leads to an epiphany. For me it's fishing for bass with the hope of catching a big one and winning a tournament. While some days are less exciting than others, I appreciate the peacefulness of the moment and the clarity of thought it engenders.

Suddenly, I had a lot more time. Like millions of others, I had just been laid off from my job. After spending some downtime recovering from hernia surgery, I decided to retire and hang up the proverbial gone fishing sign—not with the intention of thinking about some big problem but rather to actually fish! But instead of catching the big one, I ended up writing a book.

Expecting to spend my career filling prescriptions and counseling patients, I never imagined that a pharmacy degree would lead to such a satisfying career in the pharmaceutical industry. In pharmacy school, I even wrote an editorial accusing those who went into the industry of having sold out their education and profession to corporate America.

Let there be no mistake about it. I am eternally grateful to the industry for providing me with a satisfying career, lasting friendships, and financial security. I love the industry's ability to solve problems and the value it creates by finding innovative new drugs that can ameliorate and (in the case of many antibiotics and cancer drugs) actually cure diseases and save lives.

After reading this book, readers may wonder why I am so critical of an industry that has been so good to me. No, I do not feel betrayed, I do not hold a grudge, and I was not interested in writing an exposé of industry wrongdoing. However, I am frustrated by the inexcusable mistakes, poor decisions, and shortsighted thinking that have compromised the public's trust in the industry and tarnished its reputation.

As the industry struggles with depleted pipelines, slowing revenue growth, and rising market expectations for better products at lower prices, an overzealous healthcare market is looking to constrain the industry for past indiscretions. I did not intend to dwell on these indiscretions, but I tried to use them as proof of a dysfunctional industry, to identify their root causes, and to learn from them in order to help create a more prosperous future. In short, I fear that without change the industry will find it increasingly difficult to secure the resources needed to find the treatments and cures we will all need at some point in our lives.

I hope that those who read this book will better understand the challenges the industry faces and develop informed, practical, realistic expectations for the future. It is my hope that this book will also provide some guidance for what needs to be done, stimulate a different way of thinking about the industry's business model, and inspire those who can make the necessary changes to have the courage to take action.

Yes, I have hope. In the midst of market and industry turmoil, I envision a future in which scientific integrity helps reestablish market trust and companies intensify their search for new drugs that will prevent and perhaps even cure those diseases that end so many lives prematurely. It is with this vision and hope that I wrote this book.

I want to thank Mark Engelhart, Peter Frishauf, Jeanette Fritzky, Jim Patchen, and Tom Schwei for taking the time to review the manuscript and provide many worthwhile suggestions. I also want to thank Dr. Susan Rosenthal for an outstanding editing job and the critical input that only someone who has actually practiced medicine can provide. The opinions expressed in this book and any errors that remain are mine. I also want to thank Monica Willson for her design and layout expertise, and Tanya Leonello for her beautiful cover art. I extend a special note of thanks to Brian Green, who provided me with much guidance and support as he labored to help make this book a reality. I don't think I could have done this without his help.

Finally, I want to thank my wife, Mary, who suffered through far too many of my proclamations of "one more draft and I think it's done!" Now, it finally is.

Michael G. Wokasch
June 2010

Chapter 1
Introduction

The pharmaceutical industry, a seemingly modern institution, actually had its origins thousands of years ago when primitive healers concocted potions derived from natural products to treat the illnesses and wounds of family members and fellow tribesmen. Over the centuries, virtually every society has recognized the special expertise of those individuals who could formulate medications by mixing together the proper ingredients in the correct dosages to achieve the desired therapeutic effects. From primitive healers to neighborhood pharmacists in more modern times—many of whom were affectionately known as "doc"—local healers have always regarded the patient's health as their top priority. Society, for its part, has always valued the ability to craft medicines to mitigate the discomfort of illnesses and cure diseases and has held those with these talents in high regard and rewarded them handsomely.

Advances in science and medicine during the twentieth century provided the foundation from which the pharmaceutical industry was able to grow rapidly over a relatively short period of time. In the past few decades, improvements in drug discovery chemistry and our understanding of the pathophysiology of disease at the molecular level have resulted in the development of unprecedented numbers of medications that reduce suffering and cure diseases (think antibiotics, cholesterol-lowering agents, and cancer drugs). The quest to discover and develop innovative new drugs to treat and cure disease is the financial engine that drives the pharmaceutical industry, a global business with forecasted sales of over $825 billion in 2010.[1] The United States is one of the largest and most profitable pharmaceutical markets ($300 billion in sales in 2009)[2] in the world and has been a global industry bellwether for the past fifty years; it will be the focus of this book.

Today, the search for new drugs is an extremely sophisticated process involving high-tech and arcane tools such as computer-assisted molecular modeling, nuclear magnetic resonance imaging of protein structures, and an array of genomics- and proteomics-based screening assays.* Drug researchers also employ elaborately designed dosage formulations to optimize the pharmacokinetic profiles of drugs for precise dosing and delivery into the body so that they reach the appropriate site at effective but safe concentrations. Newer scientific and medical advances such as nanotechnology, stem cells, and gene therapy, while still in their infancy, add to the hope of cures for diseases previously considered untreatable death sentences. And while the availability of more and better products has led to the explosive growth of global pharmaceutical companies, the delivery of healthcare has also evolved and continues to do so in terms of how the market (e.g., government agencies, managed care organizations, hospitals, and private insurers) determines which medications to make available to patients at what cost. Unfortunately, the unintended consequences of pharmaceutical industry growth have compromised the traditional industry business model and put it in conflict with evolving market expectations. Eventually, the industry must fundamentally change how it does business to succeed in a more demanding environment where patients and healthcare providers have access to more information and payers and regulators play an increasingly larger role.

Despite the astounding technological advances that have occurred in medicine during the past fifty years, the need for disease-altering and curative treatments has not diminished. Human beings are now living longer than ever before; according to the National Center for Health Statistics, the life expectancy for males born in 2006 is estimated to be 75.1 years and for females 80.2 years.[3] Unfortunately, the aging process is accompanied by a host of illnesses and diseases (many of which are chronic and incurable) that underscore the continuing need for new therapeutic agents. Even if cures were found for the two hundred or so cancers that afflict humans, as well as Alzheimer's disease, diabetes, and many other debilitating conditions, millions of people would continue to hold out hope for therapeutic interventions that extend natural life expectancy through the use of pharmaceuticals,

* Genomics is the study of genes (segments of DNA that code for proteins) including their structure and function, while proteomics is the study of proteins (which are the actual "workhorses" in cells) including their molecular configuration and function.

vaccines, stem cells, nutriceuticals, or some other as yet to be discovered treatment option. And, at this point, the pharmaceutical industry (which includes biotechnology companies) represents the best hope for discovering and developing these new treatments into commercially available products for widespread use.

Unfortunately, drug development has not kept pace with the need for innovative new treatments; drug pipelines have dwindled recently, few truly innovative products are being introduced into clinical practice, and revenue growth in the pharmaceutical industry has slowed. At the same time, diminished public trust due to a host of missteps by the industry has led to intensified legislative and regulatory oversight and increased punitive litigation. This recent history is the backdrop for an industry that currently faces even more daunting challenges: looming patent expirations on billion-dollar blockbuster products, wholesale substitution of generic drugs for branded products, and intensifying pricing pressures. Add to these financial challenges the complexities of a fast-changing healthcare market and the uncertainties surrounding healthcare reform, and it is clear that pharmaceutical companies must change their business practices if they are to survive and prosper going forward.

A major premise of this book is that the rapid pace of advances in science and medicine combined with fast-changing healthcare market dynamics has created an increasingly complex environment for the pharmaceutical industry. The industry's complexity, along with its unbridled pursuit of revenue growth and profits to satisfy the expectations of "Wall Street" and secure personal financial gain for executives, has led to a series of missteps that are at the core of the industry's current state of dysfunction. Despite producing historically healthy profits and strong cash positions, doing business the same old way is no longer viable, nor will it be tolerated. The legislation just signed into law establishing healthcare reform in the U.S. will provide some near-term upside for the industry (approximately thirty million more Americans with prescription drug coverage), but capitalizing on these changes will be more difficult for companies that remain committed to the industry's traditional business model. If pharmaceutical companies do not change the way they do business, they will not be able to compete effectively in the evolving new healthcare market.

So how did the industry arrive at its current dysfunctional state? A little history is in order. Basking in the success of robust product pipelines during the 1970s through the 1990s, the pharmaceutical industry took full advantage of an environment in which it could seemingly do no wrong. The healthcare market was inundated with thousands of sales representatives who peddled the "latest and greatest drugs" to physicians. A steady stream of new drugs including multi-billion-dollar blockbuster products, along with an intensified focus on commercialization (marketing and sales) and double-digit price increases drove revenues and profits ever higher. The pharmaceutical industry became a proverbial cash cow. Commercial success delivered an apparently endless cash flow that allowed companies to greatly increase their spending on research and development (R&D). Management, however, focused more on revenue generation, and, as a result, became less demanding of their R&D programs, settling for modest "quick to market" improvements in existing drugs rather than innovative new products.

Despite significant increases in R&D spending by pharmaceutical companies (which most would agree is a good thing), the push for innovation was undermined by an industry-wide dilution of expertise and the ease of chemically modifying existing compounds in the laboratory. These days, when promising new drugs are patented, other companies often rush to create similar but slightly modified "me too" drugs in order to capitalize on lucrative mass markets—such as hypertension[4] (high blood pressure) and hypercholesterolemia[5] (high cholesterol)—and extend their exclusive rights to the drugs they originally introduced.* While some of these "me too" drugs may have fewer side effects or improved dosing schedules (e.g., once or twice per day rather than three or four times per day), most provide little therapeutic advantage compared to the drugs that are already available to physicians and patients. Nevertheless, the ability to "pick off" even a very small share of a highly lucrative "chronic disease" market has the potential to generate substantial profits for companies.

* For example, there are now over 100 drugs on the market in the U.S. to treat hypertension. This should not be surprising given the fact that the market for anti-hypertensive drugs is projected to generate worldwide revenues of almost $30 billion per year by 2018. A similar situation exists with regard to the cholesterol-lowering drugs called statins, two of which (Lipitor® and Crestor®) generated over $16 billion in sales in the U.S. alone in 2008.

The pharmaceutical industry, with its established commercialization (sales and marketing) infrastructure and market dominance, has also been able to prolong the market exclusivity of its products by raising concerns about the quality and safety of generic drugs, thus temporarily fending off competition from these less expensive products. Despite having approved a wide range of generic drugs by the early 1990s, the Food and Drug Administration (FDA) was unable to convince patients and physicians that generic drugs were as safe and effective as branded drugs. The occasional adverse event (e.g., breakthrough seizures in patients taking generic anti-seizure medications) also reinforced physician and patient concerns regarding the quality, safety, and efficacy of generic drugs and delayed their acceptance, albeit temporarily.*

During this same period, biotechnology companies began to establish a foothold in the market with innovative protein-based (large molecules such as monoclonal antibodies) drugs for some of the more treatment-resistant diseases such as diabetes, stroke, arthritis, and cancer. These drugs were expensive to manufacture relative to traditional small molecules, but biotechnology companies were able to charge premium prices based on the uniqueness of the treatment, its superior clinical efficacy compared to what was available at the time, and, in the case of recombinant human insulin, its safety (e.g., far fewer allergic reactions) compared to traditional insulin, which is derived from the pancreases of cows and pigs.

In the midst of its successes in this challenging market, the pharmaceutical industry lost its philosophical grounding and put the financial expectations of Wall Street and personal financial gain ahead of the welfare of patients. As the cost of drug therapy increased to the point at which some patients had to decide literally whether to eat or buy their prescription medicines, the healthcare market (i.e., managed care, hospitals, insurance companies, consumers) began to fight back by instituting restrictive drug formularies, engaging in aggressive pricing negotiations through Pharmacy Benefits Managers, and developing a renewed interest

* Despite their widespread use, generic substitutions may be considered inappropriate for potentially toxic agents where the difference between an effective dose and a safe dose is small (e.g., the heart drug digoxin, anti-epileptic drugs, and the blood thinner Coumadin® all fall into this category).

in encouraging the use of cheaper generic drugs. In an attempt to appease Wall Street and investors who had become accustomed to annual growth rates of 10% or more, pharmaceutical companies responded by hiring more sales representatives and becoming much more aggressive in marketing their products. Some even resorted to increasingly desperate and at times illegal tactics including "off-label" promotion, fraudulent pricing schemes, and questionable payments and other inducements to healthcare professionals. Commercial success and "Big Pharma"* dominance in a challenging market also gave rise to a new level of industry-wide arrogance ("where else were people going to get their medicine?") that helped transform a previously supportive and grateful patient base into one that considered the industry and its high-priced drugs to be largely responsible for rising healthcare costs.

So how did this incredibly productive industry—one that employs so many highly educated people and that once enjoyed a stellar reputation—change so quickly and so dramatically? How did the industry's once robust new drug pipeline become relatively bereft of truly unique products? How could an industry that contributed so much to the health of a grateful nation come under intense scrutiny by Congress, the Justice Department, state legislatures, the private healthcare industry, the FDA, and consumers? After decades of advances, how did this once highly innovative, science-based industry become "commoditized" (many drugs, including generics, to treat the same symptoms and diseases) to the point where it now risks losing ground in the battle against such formidable diseases as cancer, diabetes, Alzheimer's disease, and life-threatening infections? It seems that decades of goodwill toward the industry for the development of treatments that reduce pain and suffering and often prolong life—from the commercialization of cortisone by Merck scientists in the 1940s to the development of highly sophisticated monoclonal antibodies such as Herceptin® (trastuzumab) that target cancer-inducing molecules today—have been squandered in a relatively few short years. What are the reasons behind the industry's rapid fall from grace? Is there a way to turn this around? Will industry research

* A somewhat pejorative nickname used to describe large pharmaceutical and biotechnology companies. In fact, the organization that represents the industry is aptly named the Pharmaceutical Research and Manufacturers of America (PhRMA).

deliver the promised innovative new products and cures that are still desperately needed? What changes do pharmaceutical companies need to make to compete effectively in the evolving new healthcare market? These are a few of the questions I will try to answer in this book.

The consequences of not resolving this situation may be catastrophic for the industry, the healthcare system, and for those patients who are in desperate need of new treatments or cures. While some critics believe that we can get along with the medicines already at our disposal, most would argue that we need a healthy pharmaceutical industry, as long as any new drugs they discover and bring to market are relatively inexpensive. Indeed, many people who enjoy a high standard of living and have easy access to healthcare may not see the critical need for a robust and healthy pharmaceutical industry, perhaps because healthy people often do not identify with those who are less healthy than they are. Indeed, this type of thinking may be one of the reasons we have continued to tolerate the lack of affordable healthcare for tens of millions of our citizens for so long. But, as demonstrated by the 2009 global H1N1 influenza pandemic, when large numbers of individuals become sick and an alarming number die, the availability of lifesaving medicine becomes increasingly important, and, in many cases, "the cost be damned." Yet few want to acknowledge or discuss the drug development challenges and substantial investments that are necessary to develop new medicines and bring them to market. Access to "experimental drugs," which may hold out the only hope for curing a disease or extending survival, becomes newsworthy only when prominent individuals become "patients." And yet, no one wants to hear the terrible news that "we have tried everything, and there is nothing more that we can do."

Many who believe that the industry is doing just fine and that it will eventually recover as it adjusts to the evolving healthcare paradigm are industry executives who have ignored the warning signs for years and continue to deny the troubled condition in which the industry now finds itself. As occurred with the near-collapse of the big financial institutions and the bankruptcy of the major auto companies, this state of prolonged denial has brought the pharmaceutical industry to the point where small incremental changes will have little sustainable effect on improving performance or mitigating the ill will fostered by decades of poor decisions.

Because of the large size of pharmaceutical companies, the magnitude and seriousness of past industry missteps, and the changes that a rapidly evolving healthcare market will bring, more dramatic interventions will be required to "right the ship."

So where do we start? In the next few chapters, I will provide some perspective on the challenges the industry has faced and identify the self-destructive behaviors that have led to the current state of dysfunction and illustrate why many of the industry's business practices need to be changed. Throughout the book, I will provide recommendations that, if implemented, can help transform pharmaceutical companies back to a favored position—one that enables them to function with integrity while carrying out the research and development programs that are vital to producing lifesaving treatments for those diseases that continue to exact a heavy toll on the human race. While these changes will be difficult and slow, the market has already demonstrated that it is more than willing to prescribe its own solutions for managing the industry and controlling the cost of drugs if pharmaceutical companies do not change the way they do business. For the industry, the implications of inaction are clear: prescription drug price controls, aggressive use of generic drugs, the requirement for proof of "comparative efficacy" superiority, and an end to influencing prescribers through traditional marketing and sales tactics. Against this backdrop, pharmaceutical companies will need a new business model to effectively participate and compete in this rapidly evolving healthcare market.

Chapter 2
Learning from the Past for a Better Future

Prior to the passage of the Pure Food and Drug Act in 1906, the United States imposed no safety or efficacy requirements for purported medicinal agents. This laxity gave rise to an entire industry that made elixirs for every ailment known to man and to the infamous "snake oil salesmen" of the 1800s. In this unregulated market, companies and individuals could make any claim about their product, regardless of how outrageous it was (e.g., Chamlee's Cancer-Specific Purifies-the-Blood Cure), manufacture it any way they pleased, and sell it at any price the market would bear.

Public concerns about the purity of food and medicines led a reluctant Congress to pass the Pure Food and Drug Act of 1906, which ultimately became the basis for the Food and Drug Administration (FDA).[1*] Although initially the FDA had very limited authority, this legislation did succeed in establishing the expectation that medicinal agents should, at the very least, be labeled correctly and not contain any known harmful ingredients. After the sulfanilamide elixir disaster in 1937, in which over 100 people died after ingesting sulfanilamide which had been dissolved in toxic diethylene glycol, Congress passed the Federal Food, Drugs, and Cosmetics Act of 1938 which strengthened the FDA, required companies to submit safety data prior to marketing their drugs, and banned false therapeutic claims. Enforcement of these new regulations was challenging, however, since definitive proof of

* Although many people believe that passage of the Pure Food and Drug Act of 1906 was the beginning of the Food and Drug Administration, its origins actually date back to 1820 when eleven physicians established the U.S. Pharmacopeia, the first compendium of standard drugs for the United States. In 1862 the Bureau of Chemistry in the Department of Agriculture became the predecessor of the FDA.

safety and therapeutic efficacy claims was difficult to establish given the state of scientific knowledge at that time. Some individuals continued to take advantage of lax FDA enforcement (and still do), marketing unproven or ineffective treatments (e.g., numerous cough and cold elixirs, Dr. Koch's injectable glyoxylide for cancer—which was nothing more than distilled water—and Harry Hoxsey's supplements and herbal treatment for cancer) to sick patients who were in desperate need of symptom relief or in search of a cure.

This state of affairs changed dramatically following the thalidomide debacle of the 1960s. Thalidomide, which was first marketed in Germany in 1957 as a sedative-hypnotic, was also used to treat morning sickness in pregnant women. At that time, most scientists did not believe that any drug could cross the placental barrier and adversely affect a developing fetus. Thousands of women around the world who had taken thalidomide gave birth to babies with very serious birth defects including shortened limbs.* Although some trial samples of thalidomide made it into the United States, an FDA reviewer by the name of Frances Oldham Kelsey refused to approve the drug, thus sparing the U.S. market from this disaster.[2] Kelsey's decision clearly demonstrated the importance of strong regulatory authority, and Congress responded by passing the Kefauver-Harris Amendment to the Federal Food, Drugs, and Cosmetics Act in 1962 (also referred to as the Drug Efficacy Amendment). This amendment required pharmaceutical companies to supply more stringent proof of safety and substantial evidence of efficacy prior to marketing a drug, restricted drug advertising to approved therapeutic uses only, and authorized FDA inspections of manufacturing facilities. Clearly, Congress realized that the free market couldn't be trusted when it came to public health and safety. While most legitimate pharmaceutical companies were already complying (more or less) with these requirements, the new legislation made it more difficult for individuals and smaller companies that were either unwilling or un-

* Interestingly, thalidomide is currently being investigated as a possible cancer treatment in non-pregnant cancer patients because of its ability to prevent endothelial cells (flat cells that line the inside of closed spaces in the body such as blood vessels) from forming new blood vessels. The process of forming new blood vessels is termed angiogenesis, and numerous cancer drugs currently on the market are angiogenesis inhibitors.

able to comply with these more challenging requirements to avoid enforcement actions.

The Drug Efficacy Amendment of 1962 marks the beginning of the modern pharmaceutical industry. Following this legislation, many companies built world-class research and development programs that produced promising new chemical entities and subjected them to rigorous clinical trials to meet the new regulatory requirements for efficacy and safety.* The goal of these science-based programs was less about generating revenue and more

* The clinical trials process, which was first described in *The Canon of Medicine* in 1025 AD, generally occurs in four phases. During Phase I (called a dose-ranging study), a new drug is given to a small number of healthy volunteers (typically 25 to 50) in an in-patient setting to determine its safety and tolerability at various doses. A Phase I trial may also include end-stage patients for whom no other treatment option exists. During Phase II, the drug is tested in a larger number of patients (up to 300) in a continuation of the Phase I trial and to obtain preliminary efficacy data. The results of a Phase II trial are critical in determining whether to proceed with a Phase III trial. During a Phase III trial, the drug is usually administered to thousands of patients (although the actual number may be considerably less) in many different test sites in an effort to establish efficacy and safety as compared to a "standard treatment" for the disease being studied. Phase III trials are randomized and controlled so that neither the patient nor the investigator knows which treatment is being administered to which patient. These trials are the most time consuming and expensive to conduct but are the backbone of any regulatory submission (called a New Drug Application, or NDA) to the FDA. During a Phase IV trial (also known as a post-marketing surveillance trial), the company collects additional safety data for a new drug once it has been approved by the FDA. This phase may be required by the FDA as part of the drug approval process or may be undertaken by the company on its own. During a post-marketing surveillance trial, data collected from a larger number of patients than included in the Phase III trial may trigger the addition of warnings about adverse reactions and side effects to the label or the imposition by the FDA of more restrictive limitations on use. The time required for a drug to be approved varies, but currently it can take up to eight years for a cancer drug to receive FDA approval at an estimated cost to the company of as much as $1 billion. A recent designation for an exploratory trial based on the FDA's 2006 Guidance and Exploratory Investigational New Drug Studies is a Phase 0 trial. In a Phase 0 trial, also known as a human micro-dosing study, sub-therapeutic doses of a drug are administered to a small number of human subjects to determine whether the drug behaves in humans the way it does in preclinical (animal) studies. Because sub-therapeutic doses are used, the trial does not generate safety or efficacy data. Pharmaceutical companies often use the results of Phase 0 studies as the basis to either proceed or not proceed with development of a drug candidate.

about finding and developing safe compounds that would fill the unmet medical needs of patients. All data from safety and efficacy testing were formally submitted as a New Drug Application to the Food and Drug Administration for review and possible approval. While corporate decision-makers and investors clearly understood that it would take more time and money to discover, develop, and commercialize a new product, they expected to reap substantial financial rewards during the remaining period of market exclusivity, which could last as long as a decade, if not more, after the drug finally reached the market.* They also knew that it would take time and be equally challenging for competitive products to make it through this process. Back then, long-term plans were truly long-term and were not driven by quarterly financial results, and the expectations of Wall Street took a back seat to the pressing needs of running a company that depended on getting the science right and meeting the needs of patients.

Expertise in the basic sciences of biology and chemistry and a keen understanding of how a particular step in a metabolic pathway might lead to a treatment for a particular disease were the foundation of discovery research. New compounds were discovered by matching the activity of naturally occurring or synthetically produced molecules against a wide range of targets (e.g., bacteria, viruses, fungi, etc.) or by finding a compound that interfered with the biological process being studied. A good example of this latter approach started with the discovery by Dr. Sidney Farber that folic acid stimulated the growth of leukemia cells. This discovery eventually led to the development of several folic acid antagonists—including methotrexate—that induced temporary remissions in children with acute leukemia. Industry scientists benefited from a close working relationship with academic researchers in their attempts to understand the underlying pathophysiology of various diseases while identifying or synthesizing molecules that might become useful therapeutic interventions.

* Market exclusivity in this context means the period during which a company can market a drug without generic competition. For drugs discovered after 1989, patent protection lasts twenty years from the date the patent is applied for, but because patent applications are submitted early after discovery and well before a drug is in clinical trials, the effective life of a patent is generally between seven and twelve years, depending on how long it takes to develop the drug and obtain FDA approval.

Pharmaceutical companies developed an organizational passion for finding cures that transcended job functions, job titles, and departmental responsibilities. This mindset made for comprehensive long-term planning, disciplined R&D pipeline evaluations, careful allocation of resources, and a healthy respect for technical competence and scientific expertise. And because science drove the research, it was also an integral part of a pharmaceutical company's culture and overall image. The strength and reputation of its research and development team—which also enhanced the value of its products—became the foundation upon which its credibility with the medical community rested. A company's research reputation also fostered a culture of corporate integrity that was grounded in the ethics of medical practice and rigorous scientific investigation. As a result of this focus and commitment, by the second half of the 1990s more than thirty new molecular entities per year were being approved by the FDA, including a record high of fifty-six approvals in 1996 alone.[3]

During this period, traditional, large pharmaceutical companies focused primarily on designing and synthesizing small-molecule drugs* in the laboratory using a variety of sophisticated chemical processes. In contrast, biotechnology companies, which tended to be small start-ups, focused on using equally if not even more sophisticated recombinant DNA technology to create large-molecule proteins (e.g., insulin, monoclonal antibodies) for diagnostic or therapeutic use. In addition to their cutting-edge science, biotechnology companies fostered a fun, non-bureaucratic, entrepreneurial work environment that provided a welcome escape for those who were tired of the stodgy decision-making and bureaucratic cultures that often characterized large pharmaceutical companies. However, as more biotechnology companies brought high-margin products to market, and as traditional pharmaceutical companies ventured into the large-molecule space, the differences between these two corporate platforms blurred. In fact, the term "biopharmaceutical" is frequently used to describe companies that participate in both areas of drug development. Further blurring the distinction between these two models is the recent acquisition

* Organic compounds with a molecular weight of not more than 800 daltons (a dalton is the molecular weight of a hydrogen atom). Once ingested, these compounds pass into the small intestine and rapidly diffuse across cell membranes into the general circulation.

of biotechnology companies by large pharmaceutical companies (e.g., the acquisition of Genentech by Roche and Millennium by Takeda Pharmaceutical Co.).

Unfortunately, the era of robust product development did not last long. In retrospect, the low-hanging fruit of drug discovery (e.g., products to safely lower blood pressure and high cholesterol) may have been picked during the thirty-five-year period between 1970 and 2005. The availability of new drug development technologies also encouraged the FDA to gradually bolster the regulatory requirements for proving the safety and effectiveness of innovative new drugs. Ultimately, the need for more data acquired from more patients coupled with often changing and confusing expectations of proof of efficacy added a great deal of time and expense to the clinical development process for innovative new drugs.

During this time, researchers became adept at making slight alterations in the chemical structures of drugs to create progeny or "me-too drugs" that might have some modest competitive advantages over the parent compound. Many of these modifications were intended to rid the progeny drug of some troubling side effect or reduce its dosing schedule (e.g., from three times a day to once daily). While these molecular modifications sometimes produced me-too drugs that were better than the parent compound, their ease of development also undermined innovative product research. With an already approved parent drug providing the molecular framework for discovery and a regulatory-tested clinical development plan in place, developing additional me-too drugs became the easiest and fastest way to obtain FDA approval for a "new" (at least for the company if not the market) product. An excellent example of this strategy occurred following the FDA approval in 1987 of the synthetic antibacterial drug Cipro® (ciprofloxacin), which was based on a chemical modification of nalidixic acid. Marketed in the United States by Miles Pharmaceuticals (owned by Bayer) as a second-generation fluorinated quinolone or fluoroquinolone, ciprofloxacin was (and still is) used to treat a variety of infections.* Because of its overwhelming success (its sales in the United States during its first year on the market were over $100 million[4]), other companies got into the act and de-

* The first-generation quinolone was nalidixic acid, which was introduced in 1962 for the treatment of urinary tract infections.

veloped me-too products. In fact, over the ensuing fifteen-year period, at least twenty quinolones were introduced globally, some of which never made it to the United States or were subsequently withdrawn from the U.S. market due to safety concerns.

Long development time frames and expensive clinical trials also posed significant hurdles for generic drugs until Congress passed the Drug Price Competition and Patent Term Restoration Act in 1984 (known as the Hatch-Waxman Act).[5] This legislation allowed companies to obtain relatively quick FDA approval for generic formulations of branded drugs that had lost their patent protection. Hatch-Waxman allowed generic drug manufacturers to secure FDA approval by submitting bioequivalence data demonstrating that the absorption and distribution properties of a generic drug were similar to those of the original compound. Section 505(b)(2) of this Act allows generic drug companies to seek FDA approval based on data developed by other companies (i.e., publicly available branded company data). The Act also extended patent protection (referred to as *data exclusivity*) for proprietary new drugs for up to an additional five years to account for regulatory review time. The increased regulatory requirements for new products, however, combined with the faster route to market for generic drugs, led to a greatly reduced duration of market exclusivity for the former, further decreasing the opportunity to make profits and recover costs on newly launched proprietary products.

As patents expired on proprietary branded products, the generic drug industry began to prosper despite attempts by traditional pharmaceutical companies to stall entry of these products into the market. As the market became increasingly managed, generic drugs gradually gained market acceptance, and their dramatically lower prices drove utilization. Today, generic drugs account for well over 70% of dispensed prescriptions in the United States,[6] and can quickly erode revenues from a former proprietary branded product within months following patent expiration. Even though generics are substantially cheaper than branded medications, it would be incorrect for readers to assume that the generic drug business is not lucrative. In fact, the global market for generic drugs was $83 billion for the twelve-month period ending in September 2009 (U.S. sales were $31 billion through November).[7] Teva Pharmaceuticals, the world's largest manufacturer of generic drugs that recently announced its acquisition of Ratiopharm, a German generic drug company, posted 2009 revenues of over

$13.9 billion.[8] Even in the absence of healthcare reform, the market for generic drugs was growing as major blockbuster drugs continued to come off patent. This growth in generic drug sales has prompted many traditional pharmaceutical companies (e.g., GlaxoSmithKline, Novartis, Pfizer) to acquire generic drug companies and explore other generic drug business options in anticipation of increasing demand and as a hedge against the high cost of developing and marketing new proprietary products.

In the early years of the modern pharmaceutical industry (1970s and early 1980s), companies were smaller and there were fewer of them, and they tended to be regional in their focus. Companies that wanted to become multinational concentrated primarily on developing additional business in the United States, Europe, or Japan, depending on where the company did business in the first place (e.g., European companies expanded into the United States). These three regions constituted the market for more than 75% of the branded pharmaceutical products in the world.[9] In order to increase access to effective new treatments but also because of increasing growth expectations from investors and Wall Street, it became necessary for companies to expand into new markets despite the challenges and costs involved in doing so. Increased globalization of the industry added significant complexity to the management of these multinational companies. Along with larger operational infrastructures came new regulatory and legal compliance issues, different pricing and reimbursement policies, and intensified competitive commercialization issues that required considerable investment in local expertise.

The marketing of medicinal agents in the United States has always been a balancing act between providing healthcare professionals with factual scientific and medical information about new products and creating hype. For some years after Congress passed the Drug Efficacy Amendment of 1962, success in commercializing a pharmaceutical product was driven by the strength of the science behind the product and the ability of the sales team to communicate the science accurately and effectively to a relatively small audience of physicians. Fewer competitors in the marketplace and fewer treatment options for a particular disease made it easier for companies to develop sales and marketing programs that were based on science rather than exaggerated comparative claims. For example, before cimetidine (Tagamet®) was marketed by Smith Kline and French (SKF) in 1976, patients with peptic ulcers had few treatment options other than surgery. (Interested readers may want to read about the R&D effort by SKF scientists that ultimately led to the development of cimetidine.[10])* During this same time, generic drugs represented much less of a competitive threat to market share, and the only payer consideration was providing the best price to the government which, in the United States, consisted of the military, the Public Health Service, and the Veterans Administration.

As the industry evolved, more products were introduced to treat more diseases. The large number of drugs in the pipelines during the 1980s and 1990s meant that more companies were now in the market and more companies had to expand their infrastructures to manufacture and market these new products. The new products along with global expansion provided for healthy revenue growth, which was often maximized with double-digit price increases. High drug prices and relatively low manufacturing costs delivered gross margins that allowed for even more aggressive commercialization, larger R&D budgets, and financial security for industry employees. The consistent increases in cash flow and healthy profits led to bloated internal budgets and inefficient spending habits and ultimately provided a target for the outrage voiced by healthcare consumers over the seemingly endless and unjustified increases in prescription drug prices that continue to this day.

As the industry grew and prescription drugs began to consume a larger share of the healthcare budget (approaching 10%),[11] those paying for medical care, primarily the government (i.e., Medicare,

* Given the potential size of the peptic ulcer market, it didn't take long for other companies to get into the act. The next drug in this class (called H_2-receptor antagonists) to receive FDA approval was ranitidine (Zantac®), which was marketed by Glaxo. Although figures are not available, it is certain that Glaxo spent hundreds of millions of dollars to promote ranitidine in an effort to persuade physicians to switch patients from cimetidine to ranitidine. These promotional efforts clearly paid off because by 1988, ranitidine was the largest selling prescription drug in the world. This commercialization scenario was replayed in 1985 when Merck and Johnson & Johnson co-marketed famotidine (Pepcid®) in an effort to compete with cimetidine and ranitidine and again in 1987 when Eli Lilly marketed nizatidine (Axid®). Nizatidine was the last me-too drug in this class to receive FDA approval prior to the introduction of proton-pump inhibitors (e.g., omeprazole, lansoprazole, esomeprazole, etc.), which have a completely different mechanism of action than H_2-receptor antagonists.

Medicaid) and private health insurance companies and their prescription drug guardians (known as Pharmacy Benefits Managers, or PBMs), became increasingly involved in deciding which products would be available to their patients and how much they were willing to pay for them. The days when commercialization was achieved simply by creating market awareness and educating physicians about the benefits versus the risks of a new drug were giving way to a complex maze of bureaucratic influences on prescribing and an invisible network of gatekeepers who decided if the drug would even be covered by insurers. The pharmaceutical industry was ill-equipped to deal with these changes. In an effort to push marginally better products into this more challenging market, industry executives began hiring and deploying more salespeople. The continued revenue growth appeased Wall Street and led to financial gains for bonus-driven sales personnel and executives. What the industry really needed, however, was more innovative products that could be more easily differentiated, more market credibility, and people with the expertise and skills to successfully navigate the labyrinth of decision-makers, negotiate pricing, and ensure the appropriate use of their products in these new, more restricted environments.

The rapid advances in science and medicine combined with the organizational growth of pharmaceutical companies and the ever-changing healthcare market added increased complexity to an already challenging business. Seemingly uncontrolled growth in the industry produced a number of unintended consequences that ultimately led to the dysfunctional state the industry finds itself in today. The demand for scientific and business expertise quickly outstripped supply. The result was a cascading effect whereby an increasing number of managers who were inexperienced, incompetent, or simply arrogant were now responsible for making critical decisions for companies that were growing exponentially in an industry that was becoming more complex. Many of the decisions of these new managers ultimately turned out to be very poor and were made worse by questionable ethical behavior and moral compromises that led to an erosion of public trust and confidence in the industry.

The cumulative effect of this toxic corporate mix is the current dysfunctional state of the pharmaceutical industry and the less apparent but equally important financial distress it now faces. Fewer innovative drugs are being introduced to replace the blockbuster products that are coming off patent and being replaced with generic drugs. Companies continue to employ inefficient and expensive commercialization tactics (e.g., sales calls and direct-to-consumer ads), and government agencies are imposing increased regulatory and legislative oversight in response to questionable and sometime illegal drug company activities—all of which indicate that difficult times lie ahead. Any hope for a quick recovery is complicated by the uncertainty surrounding healthcare reform and a public that is desperately looking for ways to reduce the cost of healthcare and especially for prescription drugs.

Even in light of these changes, Big Pharma may be able to weather the current storm by virtue of its large cash holdings. Indeed, some companies will see the current financial distress of the market as a buying opportunity and will acquire smaller competitors, especially cash-strapped start-up biotech companies, while others will embrace a get-bigger strategy. Unfortunately, the recent mega-mergers (i.e., Pfizer-Wyeth, Roche-Genentech, Merck-Schering) may actually be self-destructive in the long run, because any near-term revenue or margin upside will be quickly offset by the inefficiencies and complexities involved in corporate integrations and the inherent challenges of managing these larger organizations. Even more importantly, the increased organizational size of these mega-companies will make it more difficult for them to adapt quickly to the evolving healthcare market. Indeed, in the absence of significant organizational and industry-wide retooling, the industry may become populated by a few large dinosaurs that continue to suffer from the effects of diminished R&D productivity, operational inefficiency, commoditization (i.e., marketing a number of undifferentiated products and their generic equivalents), and reduced profitability.

This phenomenon of commoditization leading to diminished profitability has already played out for antibiotics and vaccines. Challenging regulatory approval requirements, marginal product differentiation, pricing pressures, diminished profitability, and low expectations for future returns on investment resulted in the wholesale abandonment by Big Pharma of antimicrobial research over the past twenty years and a slow but progressive decline in FDA approvals.[12] Similarly, in the influenza vaccine market, reduced market opportunities, the high cost of manufacturing, pricing pressures, and the risk of product liability litigation eliminated all but two manufacturers from the U.S. market (Aventis

Pasteur and Evans Vaccines) in 2002.[13] Only after the H1N1 pandemic (swine flu) led to government vaccine purchase guarantees and other financial incentives for vaccine development was there a renewed interest in vaccine development.

The lessons from this brief history are simple:

1. The market and investors expect pharmaceutical companies to discover and market innovative new drugs that will address unmet medical needs.
2. As pharmaceutical companies become more aggressive in their commercialization efforts, the market will respond with more restrictions and regulations.
3. Consumers and insurers will seek out less expensive alternative treatments to innovative new products that are either perceived to be or actually are priced too high.
4. Rapid organizational growth results in unintended consequences that can be damaging to the company and the industry. In addition to the logistics of managing the complexities of a larger corporate entity, maintaining a high level of expertise (and integrity) becomes increasingly difficult as organizations grow.
5. Challenging or constrained market opportunities reduce the incentives for pharmaceutical companies to invest in new treatment options.

While the need for incentives remains, the healthcare market will continue to undergo dramatic changes, with increasing expectations for pharmaceutical companies set against a backdrop of a greater focus on the cost of drugs and more restrictions on corporate influence over decision-makers. If companies do not make the necessary changes to align themselves with this more challenging environment, the industry's future will be clouded. Restricted access to higher-priced treatments, aggressive therapeutic substitution with generic drugs, and perhaps some misguided initiatives (e.g., higher rebate expectations and shortening market exclusivity) as part of an overall effort to control and manage prescription drug prices will negatively affect the profitability of the industry. While these tactics may deliver some near-term cost-savings, they will occur at the expense of reduced long-term investment in new and potentially even more cost-effective medicines. There is an urgent need to balance the necessary investment in pharmaceutical R&D with the market's expectation of affordable if not cheap drugs. To date, however, the market has been relentless in its pursuit of lower drug prices while demanding even more effective products in the face of increased regulatory and legislative controls on the industry. As long as the industry continues to maintain that price is merely a reflection of the high cost of research and the risks associated with drug development—even for marginally differentiated products—the opportunity to achieve balance in this relationship will continue to diminish, and we will all suffer, if not now, then in the not-too-distant future.

Is there a way to achieve balance and reconcile what appear to be diametrically opposing expectations? It is this author's belief that reconciliation is not only possible but essential if the pharmaceutical industry is to regain the public's trust and sustain the profitability it needs to survive.

Chapter 3
An Increasingly Dysfunctional Industry

Over the past few decades, economic conditions have produced dramatic changes in healthcare delivery and, in particular, in prescription drug marketing and purchasing. During this period, the pharmaceutical industry has managed to alienate almost every group with its organizational arrogance, aggressive (and sometimes illegal) marketing tactics, questionable scientific integrity, and operational missteps. Although healthy cash reserves have helped it weather the current economic storm, at least until now, the prosperous days of the pharmaceutical industry as we have known it appear to be numbered.* Without significant and sweeping changes, pharmaceutical companies will struggle to compete effectively in the evolving healthcare environment. Unfortunately, the industry appears to be in denial regarding its current state of dysfunction, best exemplified by pharmaceutical CEOs who publicly try to rationalize the strategic basis for mega-mergers, acquisitions, and organizational changes (mostly lay-offs and departmental restructurings). The list of issues the industry is ignoring is long and includes its disappointing R&D programs, repeated lapses in corporate and scientific integrity, and blatant disregard for ethical as well as regulatory and legal considerations when commercializing products, all of which have had a corrosive influence on public trust and confidence. The current state of the industry can be assessed by looking at the following major indicators of dysfunction.

* A recent (April 2010) Moody's investor service report noted that debt in the pharmaceutical industry was rising (up 117% from 2006 to 2009) and growth in debt outstripped growth in cash. Moody's rating of the industry has declined to reflect higher operating and financial risks.

Diminishing R&D productivity: Fewer innovative product approvals

During the past twenty years, productivity in drug discovery and development has declined steadily, resulting in fewer FDA (Food and Drug Administration) approvals and commercial launches of innovative new products. On average, the FDA approved thirty or more new drugs a year from the late 1970s through the 1990s, but approvals have diminished fairly consistently since a high in 1996 when fifty-six drugs were approved (Figure 3-1). Ironically, this decline has come despite huge outlays by the industry; by some estimates total industry R&D spending now exceeds $65 billion a year compared to less than $2 billion annually in the 1970s.[1] The top twenty pharmaceutical companies each now spend over $1 billion a year on R&D, while the top five companies each spend over $5 billion a year.[2] The industry also benefits from government investments in basic research ($30.5 billion in 2009)[3] at the National Institutes of Health that often leads to drug targets or drug candidates that can either be licensed or acquired. If innovative new products are the lifeblood of the industry, the depleted pipelines of today should be very troubling to pharmaceutical executives, investors, and patients alike, especially given the high levels of R&D spending over the past decade.

Figure 3-1. Number of drugs approved by the FDA, 1996-2009. Adapted by permission from Macmillan Publishers Ltd. (Nature Reviews Drug Discovery), volume 9, pp 89-92, 2010.

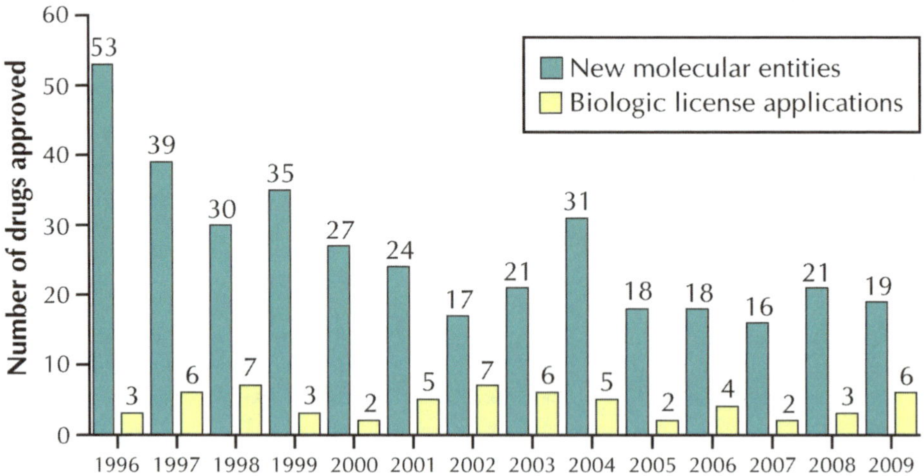

Slowing revenue growth

As a result of diminishing pipelines and fewer differentiated products, the industry faces increasingly challenging growth prospects. Pharmaceutical companies simply do not have the product pipelines to fill the huge revenue gaps they now face as several multi-billion-dollar blockbuster products (e.g., Lipitor®, Plavix®, Viagra®) are expected to lose their patent-protected market exclusivity in the U.S. over the next few years.[4] Revenue growth has actually been slowing even before taking into account the impact of blockbuster product patent expirations. While the global pharmaceutical market will approach $825 billion in 2010,[5] during the past decade revenue growth has gradually declined in the U.S. Prior to 2000, with few exceptions, the industry was able to deliver annual revenue growth in the low to mid-teens.[6] A steady stream of new products helped drive this growth, which was further enhanced by double-digit price increases and global expansion. Despite a boost from passage of the Medicare Prescription Drug, Improvement, and Modernization Act (Medicare Part D)* in 2003, prescription drug spending has continued to decline and grew by only 1.8% in 2008.[7] This slowing in revenue growth is the result of fewer new product launches, increased competition from generic drugs, approval by the FDA to allow switching of some prescription drugs to lower-priced over-the-counter treatments (e.g., Motrin®, Prilosec®), and more modest price increases as the managed healthcare market (federal and state governments and private insurance companies) has become increasingly reluctant to pay for high-priced drugs. In an effort to combat this slowdown in growth, companies spent more on sales and marketing during this same period (reaching $12.7 billion in 2008)[8] and deployed tens of thousands of sales representatives in the field.[9]

Perhaps one of the biggest factors in the reduction of pharmaceutical company revenues has been the successful deployment of

* The Medicare Prescription Drug Improvement and Modernization Act, which was passed into law on December 8, 2003, and went into effect on January 1, 2006, established a new Part D Voluntary Prescription Drug Benefit Program. The pharmaceutical industry benefits from this federal program, which makes prescription drugs more affordable for Medicare beneficiaries through government-supported prescription drug plans available to traditional Medicare beneficiaries and participants in Medicare Advantage plans.

various tactics by government and private insurance companies to decrease the cost of drug therapy. Drug formularies, discounts in the form of rebates (payments back to the purchaser), and restrictive reimbursement policies have been very effective at reducing prescription drug costs. A drug formulary is a list of prescription drugs that will be paid for by the patient's insurance company, by Medicare, or by state Medicaid programs. These formularies also determine the amount that patients will have to pay (the co-pay) to partially offset the high cost of branded products. In the most restrictive cases, no reimbursement will be made for a drug not on formulary, leaving the patient with the option of paying for it directly or having the physician prescribe another drug that is on the list. Restricted formularies also provide insurers with significant leverage to negotiate price and encourage the use of generic drugs. Products not on formularies tend not to be prescribed; their availability is limited at local wholesalers and pharmacies, and they are sold only to the few patients who are willing and able to pay for them. For pharmaceutical companies, having drugs on formularies with minimal restrictions, nominal rebates, and attractive reimbursement terms (no or low patient co-pays) is critical for product use and revenue generation.

The complexities of treatment options and the potential for cost savings led to the birth of an entire industry of Pharmacy Benefits Managers. Their purported expertise in assessing available drug therapies, negotiating discounted pricing, and facilitating transaction logistics may justify their role in helping healthcare plans reduce the cost of drug therapy. Pharmacy Benefits Managers also encourage and facilitate generic substitution (thus replacing branded proprietary drugs) while controlling the ability of pharmaceutical sales and marketing efforts to influence the use of particular products by healthcare professionals.

Resorting to illegal marketing and sales tactics

As the federal government became an ever larger purchaser of prescription drugs, reducing the cost of drug therapy became an even higher priority. Increased government oversight led to unwanted publicity regarding industry pricing policies and commercialization tactics. The federal government began requiring manufacturers to provide rebates and disclose and report quarterly pricing information. An elaborate and often confusing set of calculations was required, including information on how the retrospective average selling price (ASP) was determined and reported. In addition, many states enacted their own legislation for calculating and reporting prices that emulated but was often significantly different from the federal government's definitions, calculations, and reporting requirements.

These measures not only provided greater transparency for pricing policies but also allowed state and federal agencies to use price reporting discrepancies as a basis for fraud claims litigation. While the complexities of price reporting certainly contributed to inadvertent mistakes, a number of cases suggested companies were using this complex web of price reporting to increase sales and garner higher margins. As expected, it did not take state attorneys general long to realize that these indiscretions could become a revenue source, with hundreds of millions of settlement dollars contributing to an indirect reduction in the cost of drug therapy for their financially strapped state healthcare programs.

Healthcare market cost control tactics put additional pressure on pharmaceutical companies as they struggled to deliver the double-digit growth that Wall Street expected and even demanded. With fewer innovative breakthrough products in the pipeline and increased scrutiny by formularies of new products that offered only marginal therapeutic benefits over existing ones, many companies became uncharacteristically aggressive in their commercialization strategies. Some moved from merely pushing the regulatory envelope to embracing tactics that were highly questionable from a legal perspective. What the industry did not anticipate from the legal discovery process (the ability to request previously unavailable confidential corporate documents related to the initial lawsuit) and resultant pricing fraud litigation were the revelations of additional dubious and unethical commercialization tactics that ultimately became the basis for further litigation.

Based on the belief that a reduction in pharmaceutical advertising and promotion expenses (often hundreds of millions of dollars for a single drug) would translate into lower prescription drug prices, government agencies became aggressive in pursuing fraud and false claims litigation in an effort to extract multimillion-dollar settlements and fines from pharmaceutical companies. Often initiated by whistleblower (usually an employee) claims of corporate wrongdoing such as off-label promotion (which is illegal and involves actively promoting a drug for non-FDA-approved uses*), the Department of Justice, the Federal Trade Commission, and state attorneys general found they could hold pharmaceutical companies accountable for their marketing indiscretions and effectively replaced the FDA as the pharmaceutical industry's regulatory enforcer.

Successful litigation against pharmaceutical companies led to negative media coverage and an unsympathetic market, which eventually resulted in wholesale erosion of pharmaceutical industry credibility. Many of the tactics that came to light were not just isolated cases inspired by maverick employees but rather well-orchestrated programs carried out by some of the largest and most admired companies in the industry. As the sordid details of these cases were disclosed, there was a steady deterioration in the goodwill the industry had accrued over the decades as it endured a seemingly endless course of litigation regarding pricing fraud and highly questionable commercialization tactics. So just how bad and how widespread were these industry missteps?

In one of the earliest whistleblower cases, TAP Pharmaceuticals (a joint venture formed in 1977 between Abbott Laboratories and Takeda Pharmaceutical Company, a Japanese corporation.) was accused of defrauding Medicare and Medicaid of hundreds of millions of dollars throughout the 1990s in a scheme involving its drug Lupron® (leuprolide acetate). Lupron is a relatively expensive injectable drug used to treat prostate cancer and other urologic and gynecologic disorders. Because it is administered in an office setting, physicians can bill Medicare and Medicaid for the cost of the drug. The company was accused of helping to defraud the government by artificially inflating the average wholesale price† (AWP) of the drug and advising physicians to use the inflated AWP rather than the discounted acquisition price (the price the physician actually paid) when seeking reimbursement from the government. This meant more money for those physicians who engaged in this practice and increased revenues for TAP at the expense of taxpayers.

---

* Although pharmaceutical companies cannot legally market or promote their drugs for non-FDA-approved indications, physicians are free to prescribe a drug for *any* disease or condition once it is FDA-approved.

† The AWP was often used as a basis for determining reimbursement, including reimbursement for Medicare and Medicaid programs. AWP has now been replaced by ASP (average selling price), which is defined as the average price based on actual sales transactions.

An investigation into this case led to disclosure of other questionable marketing and sales tactics involving TAP and Lupron. The Department of Justice characterized TAP's use of so-called consulting fees, educational grants, and all-expenses paid trips to golf and ski resorts as kickbacks and bribes to physicians in return for their use of the drug. After several years of litigation, this high-profile case was settled in 2001, with TAP agreeing to plead guilty and pay $875 million to resolve criminal charges and civil liabilities related to this case.[10] Despite the fact that this was the highest criminal fine ever imposed on any healthcare company in the United States up to that time, it was small potatoes compared to the billions in revenue generated by the illegal scheme. The company subsequently paid an additional $150 million in 2005 to compensate consumers who paid inflated prices due to the AWP manipulation.[11]

Another well-publicized example of commercialization litigation by the U.S. Justice Department involved the off-label promotion of Neurontin® (gabapentin). Neurontin was initially marketed by Warner-Lambert (acquired by Pfizer in 2007) and was FDA-approved to treat a special kind of seizure disorder that affects a relatively small patient population. The case alleged that Warner-Lambert had planned and orchestrated a comprehensive marketing and sales campaign designed to sell the drug for a variety of unapproved indications: bipolar disorder, pain, migraine headaches, and drug and alcohol withdrawal, all of which represented a significantly larger market opportunity than the approved seizure indication.* Obtaining FDA approval for unapproved uses (which by no means was a certainty) would have required years of clinical studies and a sizeable investment by the company. By circumventing the FDA approval process, the off-label promotion reportedly drove sales to $2.7 billion in 2003, with as much as 90% of revenues derived from off-label uses.[12] Warner-Lambert ultimately pled guilty and paid a fine of $430 million to resolve criminal charges and civil liabilities.[13] Viewed in the context of the enormous sales generated by this scheme, however, the fine was a small price to pay for these tactics.

* Physicians can legally prescribe drugs for unapproved indications and often do so because certain drugs may provide benefits for indications other than those approved by the FDA. Furthermore, some patients fail to respond or are unable to tolerate approved products.

In yet another whistleblower case that concluded in the fall of 2009, Pharmacia & Upjohn Co., a subsidiary of Pfizer, agreed to pay $1.3 billion for misbranding Bextra® (valdecoxib), a non-steroidal anti-inflammatory drug approved in 2001 for the treatment of mild pain associated with rheumatoid arthritis. Pfizer also agreed to pay an additional $1 billion to resolve civil and criminal liabilities arising from the off-label promotion of the drug, as well as for illegal promotion of several other drugs including the antibiotic Zyvox® (linezolid).[14] The government alleged that Pfizer provided kickbacks as part of a scheme to encourage physicians to prescribe the drugs for off-label uses (some of which the FDA had declined to approve due to safety concerns). In the Bextra® case, the government alleged that sales representatives were instructed by the marketing team to promote the drug for off-label uses including the treatment of acute pain and post-surgical pain and at dosages the FDA had not approved.[15]*

In another recent whistleblower case, various federal and state agencies accused AstraZeneca of allegedly marketing its anti-psychotic drug Seroquel® (quetiapine) for a wide range of off-label uses during the period 2001 through 2006. The company was also accused of "improperly and unduly" influencing the content of company-funded continuing medical education programs and paying doctors to give talks about the drug for unapproved uses. As a result of these marketing efforts, the company was accused of causing false claims for payment to be submitted to Medicare, Medicaid, and the Veterans Administration. Although the company denied the allegations, it agreed to pay $520 million to settle the suit. As in the other cases, however, the fine was a small price to pay for a drug that had 2009 sales of $4.87 billion.[16]

In the most recent whistleblower case to date, Novartis (which acquired Chiron in 2006) agreed to pay $72.5 million to settle charges of off-label promotion of TOBI®, an inhaled formulation of the antibiotic tobramycin.[17] This product was FDA-approved for the treatment of the chronic lung infections that often accompany cystic fibrosis, an inherited disease that leads to the production of thick mucus in the gastrointestinal and respiratory tracts. The U.S. Department of Justice charged that as a result of the off-label promotion, which allegedly occurred from 2001 to 2006, Novartis

* Pfizer acquired Bextra® when it purchased Pharmacia in 2003. Bextra was withdrawn from the U.S. market in 2005 due to safety concerns.

(and Chiron) caused false claims to be submitted to various federal healthcare programs.

The cases against these companies were important because, like other cases that had come to light, they provided previously undisclosed insights into industry commercialization tactics and began to raise very uncomfortable questions about the relationship between the industry and prescribing physicians. In addition, these cases revealed detailed background material for litigators and state attorneys general who were looking to protect their constituents by building subsequent cases against pharmaceutical companies through the use of laws against kickbacks, fraud, and false claims. Extensive media coverage of some of these cases and others led to widespread accusations that the industry was cheating the taxpayer, stealing from the elderly, and putting profits ahead of people's health.

Putting patients at risk to increase and protect sales

Product liability has always been a significant risk factor for the industry. A major challenge for sales representatives and the companies they represent is finding the right balance when discussing the clinical benefits of a product versus its possible side effects and adverse reactions. The market has become less forgiving of pharmaceutical companies that fail to properly disclose the hazards associated with the use of their products. Many product liability cases have been based on allegations of intentional nondisclosure or misleading, carefully crafted (often in conjunction with public relations firms and advertising agencies*) communiqués that were part of ongoing attempts to ensure that potentially damaging safety data did not interfere with sales.

One of the more highly publicized product liability cases involved a diet drug nicknamed fen-phen, a combination of fenfluramine or dexfenfluramine and phentermine that was marketed by American Home Products, or AHP (which later became Wyeth). For years these products (fenfluramine, dexfenfluramine,

* An entire industry exists to help pharmaceutical companies advertise and promote their products. See Chapter 10 for an in-depth look at pharmaceutical marketing and the role that marketers play in getting the word out about their drugs.

and phentermine) had been marketed individually as diet drugs but were considered only marginally effective. In 1992, however, a single clinical study involving 121 obese patients reported that when these drugs were used in combination, patients achieved extraordinary weight loss without apparent side effects.[18] The public's obsession with a quick fix for obesity, a *TIME* magazine cover story hyping the new weight reduction option,[19] and a book dedicated to "...the Most Important Weight Loss Discovery of the Century"[20] drove an estimated six million people to try this combination. Unfortunately, the combination was later found to cause serious heart valve and lung damage in some patients, and the products were withdrawn from the market in 1997. The media, which had helped champion this once-popular weight-loss treatment, subsequently highlighted the serious questions about the safety of the combination, prompting patients to join in massive class-action lawsuits, while tens of thousands of others filed individual lawsuits. The underlying allegation for many of these cases was that AHP knew and failed to adequately warn physicians and patients about the potential for serious adverse reactions with the drug combination. AHP settled the majority of cases by establishing the AHP Diet Drug Settlement Trust with $3.75 billion after having already paid out a reported $13 billion to defend itself.[21] While these are staggering sums of money, they amounted to an average of less than $2800 for each of the estimated six million patients who tried the drug.

A more recent case involving Ketek® (telithromycin), approved in 2004 and marketed by Sanofi-Aventis for the treatment of community-acquired respiratory tract infections, triggered heightened concern about scientific integrity in the industry and questionable activities on the part of the FDA related to approval of the product. Despite the drug's potential to cause serious side effects, including fatal liver toxicity, the company appeared to have covered up damaging information about the drug—information which the FDA seemed to ignore despite reviewing the drug on three separate occasions, even though concerns were raised by its own staff. Congressional testimony by the clinical study monitor[22]* and others suggested that the company knew (or should have known) about investigator fraud in one of its primary safety studies

* The clinical study monitor is responsible for ensuring that the study is carried out according to the established protocol.

(referred to as study 3014) and alleged that the company knowingly submitted falsified data to the FDA. The Senate Finance Committee accused the FDA of failing to perform due diligence when reviewing the new drug application, knowingly presenting the falsified safety data to an FDA advisory committee, and ignoring safety concerns raised by experts, including its own.[23] Not surprisingly, this case and the accompanying negative publicity revealed the apparently high level of pharmaceutical company influence over the drug approval process and cast serious doubts about the integrity of pharmaceutical company research as well as the objectivity of FDA drug review procedures.

In another case that was concluded in May, 2007, Purdue Frederick (an affiliate of Purdue Pharma) pled guilty to charges of making false statements that minimized the addictive properties, abuse potential, and potential for withdrawal symptoms of OxyContin® (timed-release oxycodone). OxyContin, a powerful narcotic for the treatment of moderate to severe pain, is similar to morphine in terms of its addictive potential. A federal investigation concluded there was a long-term revenue maximization scheme based on the illegal promotion of OxyContin by counseling and training sales representatives to make false and misleading statements to healthcare professionals. This illegal activity not only enhanced sales but allegedly led to more cases of addiction to OxyContin that, for many, may have contributed to their deaths.[24] In this case, several former executives of Purdue Frederick pled guilty to felony misbranding (a regulatory/legal term for making false or misleading statements or statements that are inconsistent with FDA-approved label claims for a product) of OxyContin and agreed to personally pay $34.5 million in fines, while Purdue Frederick itself agreed to pay more than $600 million in penalties and restitution. One of the prosecutors was quoted as saying that "Purdue (Frederick) put its desire to sell OxyContin above the interests of the public."[25]

The cases described above represent just a few examples that provided disturbing insights into the dark side of industry commercialization tactics that had long been suspected but were only now being revealed. Litigation-driven access to company records and files has continued to provide plaintiffs with opportunities to bring additional cases alleging illegal commercialization tactics, scientific misconduct, falsification of data, misleading scientific interpretation of findings, intentional minimization of risks, and sometimes even willful non-disclosure of fatal drug side effects. As a result, the public has become increasingly outraged (and rightfully so) by the industry's greed and lack of concern for patient safety. Law firms are attempting to recruit patients who may have suffered side effects or injuries from a variety of drugs for class-action lawsuits against several pharmaceutical companies. Needless to say, the resulting lawsuits not only represent huge distractions for these companies but are also costing billions of dollars in fines, settlements, and legal fees.

Erosion of trust and confidence in the industry

Another indicator of dysfunction is diminished public trust and confidence in the industry. Despite their acknowledged skills in creating positive images for their products, pharmaceutical companies have been unsuccessful in countering the effects of litigation and the resulting negative publicity. Cases continue to be prosecuted with attention-grabbing headlines that highlight corporate malfeasance and misbehavior. Furthermore, the manner in which these companies have handled the allegations has also contributed greatly to the erosion of public trust and confidence in the industry. With thousands of lawsuits still pending, it is likely that additional disclosures of questionable industry practices and allegations of inappropriate payments to healthcare providers will come to light. These revelations will, no doubt, lead to further erosion in the public's trust and confidence. Ironically, only in the context of shameless Wall Street compensation packages rewarding abject failure has the public's perception of the pharmaceutical industry improved slightly.[26]

The public will not easily or quickly forget the aggressive and sometimes illegal marketing and sales tactics, the industry's arrogance, or its demonstrated elevation of sales over concerns for patient safety. Clinical trial results that do not pass the smell test (extraordinary efficacy with minimal side effects) and the preventable deaths of some patients that likely resulted from corporate greed and negligence continue to raise serious and damaging questions about the industry's moral and ethical priorities. These are ominous signs and symptoms of a dysfunctional industry—one that needs to understand how it wound up in this position and what it must do to get back on track.

Chapter 4
Mistakes and Poor Decisions in Large Organizations

Mistakes and poor decisions are an inevitable part of business and the business cycle. In fact, they are an important part of the learning process and are essential for developing expertise and competence. In a fast-changing environment like the healthcare market, the factors and circumstances upon which decisions are based are rarely static. The changing business environment demands that both managers and organizations as a whole strive to develop good decision-making processes. While problem-solving and decision-making techniques can be acquired through education and training, there is no substitute for real-life, on-the-job experience. When combined with insightful coaching and timely feedback, experience dealing with different issues under a variety of different circumstances will provide managers with greater ability to identify options, assess their impact, and evaluate the potential consequences of various choices.

In order for business-related mistakes and poor decisions to be transformed into positive experiences, they should have limited negative consequences for the business but enough impact to provide a memorable and sound basis for future decisions. Mistakes are such an integral part of learning that training programs, business schools, and corporate development programs often create safe environments in which mistakes and poor decisions can be made without undue concern over consequences. These programs are designed to provide opportunities for experiencing various outcomes resulting from different decisions and actions while encouraging exploration and risk taking. The opportunity to think through various options, apply different actions in a variety of scenarios, manage and deal with the consequences of these decisions, and receive timely and credible feedback can accelerate the learning experience. Nevertheless, the value of mistakes and poor decisions in a learning situation can be offset when they do harm to others or threaten the survival of a business. Attentive and experienced management oversight and coaching provide sufficient autonomy for learning to take place while mitigating damaging consequences and avoiding serious harm to the business. Even this type of learning, however, can be undermined when the person responsible for the mistakes and poor decisions does not remain in a position long enough to experience their consequences.

Many of the mistakes and poor decisions (e.g., failure to disclose serious and even fatal adverse reactions, encouragement of off-label promotion, commission of pricing fraud) that have plagued the pharmaceutical industry over the past few decades most likely originated with a single person or group of people who disregarded the potential impact of their actions on patients or the company. Although the effects of these errors could have been mitigated by diligent management oversight, their magnitude suggests that they were authorized, approved, or simply ignored by management. Thus, mistakes and poor decisions made at lower levels in the organization were compounded and magnified when they went unchecked by those at higher levels in the organization. But many would maintain that these companies had well-trained managers in positions of oversight. So, how could these mistakes have occurred in the first place? And more importantly, why were they not corrected earlier, thus avoiding the negative consequences or at least diminishing the magnitude of those consequences? One of the reasons is the considerable, often overwhelming, pressure to be a team player in large organizations. Organizational strategies, plans, and decisions tend to gain collective support and momentum when they are facilitated by the more eloquent and politically savvy managers and their allies. While this organizational culture can be a positive business attribute when applied for the benefit of customers or the market, once certain trends or actions are in place, they are often extremely difficult to reverse. Questioning the collective wisdom of the group, particularly if it is being championed by someone at an executive level, can be dangerous to one's position within the organization and ultimately may lead to being labeled a non-team player. Indeed, taking a stance that is contrary to popular positions or decisions almost certainly means placing oneself in a compromised position, with potential adverse consequences for career growth and job security. However, in order for any organization—large or small—to function effectively, individuals must be able to challenge "group-think," regardless of its origin. Thus, even in organizations with well-trained, experienced employees, management must ensure that organizational culture and team-player dynamics do not foster an environment in which mistakes and poor decisions can flourish and go unchecked. While standardization of processes, enforcement of policies and procedures, and other bureaucratic control mechanisms can reduce the numbers of errors made by an organization, none of them can, or should, replace management oversight and timely intervention.

Effective management oversight can help reduce the number of mistakes as well as their magnitude, yet they will still occur, even in the best organizations. In fact, the larger the organization, the higher the probability mistakes will occur because so many business units operate independently of one another (readers may recall that a unit of American International Group (AIG) in London was responsible for writing billions of dollars in credit protection contracts that ultimately led to the near-collapse of the entire company in 2008, only to be saved by a government bailout). Even under the best of circumstances, collective poor judgment, ignorance, inexperience or inadequate expertise, unsound legal or regulatory advice, or unfamiliar circumstances can all lead to honest mistakes and poor decision-making. Even a miscalculation of risk versus reward (frequently due to limited or incomplete information) can lead to egregious mistakes and poor decisions.* Unfortunately, some of the more disturbing reasons for the poor decisions made by pharmaceutical companies over the past several decades have to do more with simple greed than anything else. These greed-driven decisions ultimately led to a blatant disregard for patient welfare, an orchestrated defiance of regulatory and legal requirements, and willful compromises in integrity.

The frequency, magnitude, and seriousness of mistakes and poor decisions are good metrics for determining the optimum manageable size for a pharmaceutical company, or any company for that matter. In this author's opinion, the size of a pharmaceutical

* Pfizer's ill-fated venture into the inhaled insulin market, which will be discussed in Chapter 11, is an excellent example of unchecked organizational "group-think" and miscalculation of risk versus reward.

company should be directly proportional to the ability of the organization and its managers to mitigate the number, magnitude and seriousness of mistakes and poor decisions that are potentially damaging to patients, the company, and the industry. As will be discussed later, the expertise, competency, and integrity of *all* of its employees will ultimately determine the manageable size for any company.

Chapter 5

In a Complex Business Environment, Size Really Does Matter

Recent advances in science and medicine combined with a changing healthcare market have created an increasingly complex business environment for pharmaceutical companies. In response, the industry has accelerated organizational growth, including the pursuit of mega-mergers (combining two large companies into one extremely large company). But, rapid organizational growth carries with it unintended consequences; the difficulty of managing these large organizations makes them more vulnerable to mistakes and poor decisions in an industry that, by its very nature, is already complicated.

For decades, the growth rate of a company has been viewed as one of the single most important indicators of business success. Many economists insist on the need for growth; investors and Wall Street analysts applaud growth, and financial publications often focus on fast-growing companies, extolling their merits and declaring them high achievers and business success stories. Indeed, over the years, growth and growth prospects have been one of the biggest drivers of gains in stock market investment models. While most would agree that growth is important, many fail to distinguish between revenue growth and organizational growth. Revenue and earnings growth allow a company to invest in the future while rewarding investors and providing operational flexibility and financial stability in challenging times. Growth in profits can also increase the opportunity for career and personal financial success for employees. Unfortunately, revenue and earnings growth usually requires a commensurate increase in organizational growth. The addition of people and infrastructure can significantly increase organizational complexity, foster inefficiencies, dilute expertise, and reduce the chances for diligent management oversight. From an organizational standpoint, there seems to be a size (not necessarily determined by revenue) at which a company reaches its optimal, sustainable performance level. Beyond this optimal size, the complexities and logistics of managing an organization that is too large push it to a point of diminishing returns and ultimately to self-destruction. When companies exceed this size threshold across an entire industry, that industry will begin to sow the seeds of its own destruction. This scenario was recently illustrated with the collapse of Bear Stearns, Lehman Brothers, and AIG and the bankruptcy of General Motors. This author believes that many pharmaceutical companies have similarly exceeded their optimal organizational size and are now too big. Ironically, large pharmaceutical companies that reach this point of diminished productivity (e.g., Pharmacia-Upjohn, Warner-Lambert, Schering-Plough) tend to be acquired by larger companies; the larger company typically retains the core expertise and product value of the acquired company while dismantling its remaining infrastructure.

So what does "too big" mean? Quite simply, too big in the context of the pharmaceutical business means that a company's organizational complexity overwhelms its ability to identify clear lines of accountability, to function efficiently and effectively, and to provide diligent management oversight. It means the company's talent pool is no longer able to provide the products and services that are necessary to meet the needs of its customers. It means executives have lost touch with their employees and, more importantly, have become disconnected from their customer base. It means executives are so isolated from reality that their concept of a successful business strategy is based on balance sheet maintenance, the satisfaction of Wall Street expectations, and the creation of personal wealth. It also means there is little organizational guidance for, or protection from, individuals who have lost their moral and ethical compass, making the organization vulnerable to employees who are willing or tempted to push the legal and regulatory envelope in an effort to climb the corporate ladder or achieve personal financial gain.

This notion of being too big is not unique to the pharmaceutical industry. It applies to most companies, industries, and organizations. Large auto companies (now even Toyota!), banks and financial institutions, airlines, insurance companies, and government agencies all have demonstrated that there is a point at which they become operationally too large to ensure sustained functional efficiency and effectiveness. In the fall of 2008 and continuing into 2009, one of the reasons given by government officials and others for providing a taxpayer bailout (via the Troubled Asset Relief Program) to AIG, financial institutions, and automobile companies was that these entities were "too big to fail" because of the cumulative impact (consequences) their failure would have on the U.S. and global economies. In a rapidly changing market, the challenges of being too big increase substantially, and negative consequences begin to dwarf any economies of scale or real value created.

Many pharmaceutical companies have simply become too big too fast and have experienced a multitude of unintended consequences as a result of this hypergrowth. As the industry grew, more people with industry, functional, and scientific/medical expertise were needed within these fast-growing companies and within an industry which now had more companies than ever before. This rapid organizational growth led to a dilution of available expertise across the industry, which led to diminished productivity in R&D, and a delayed negative impact on the introduction of new molecular entities (see Figure 5-1). This dilution of expertise also led to reduced operational efficiencies, and abusive (and, in some instances, illegal) marketing and sales tactics. Inexperienced management and insufficient oversight helped create an environment in which mistakes and poor decisions went unchecked, resulting in ineffective, delayed, or in many cases, complete absence of management intervention that might have enhanced performance or put an end to the inappropriate activities. Some pharmaceutical companies tried to downplay or cover up their mistakes and poor decisions with the same ethical and moral lapses in personal and corporate integrity that led to the types of litigation described in chapter 3.

Managers in fast-growing companies often discuss the need for a company to reach or maintain critical mass, or the organizational size that is sufficient to accomplish the intended results, be they in research, manufacturing, commercialization, or operations. Reaching critical mass in business means that the support resources and infrastructure are sufficient to deliver the products or services promised. Clearly, one researcher alone cannot develop a drug, one salesperson cannot call on all healthcare professionals who might prescribe a drug, and one journal ad will not reach all

Figure 5-1. The number of new molecular entities (NMEs) approved by the FDA versus growth in the pharmaceutical industry from 1950 through 2006. Adapted by permission from Macmillan Publishers Ltd. (Nature Reviews Drug Discovery), volume 8, pp 959-968, 2009.

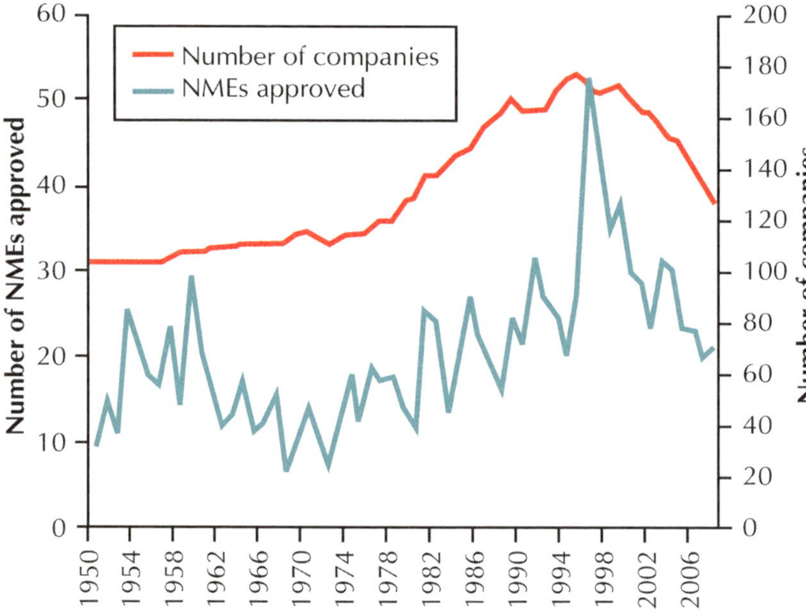

members of an intended audience. Although achievement of critical mass will not ensure success, businesses must still reach a critical mass in order to be efficient, effective, and successful.

Strong balance sheets and robust cash flows allowed the pharmaceutical industry to take the concept of critical mass to an extreme, breaching the point of diminishing returns. Supported by a strategic plan and aggressive revenue forecasts, the need for critical mass was often the basis for securing approval for progressively larger budgets and more people. In some instances this was done in an effort to create a competitive advantage, while in others it merely served to build organizational empires (the more people reporting to a particular individual, the greater the budget needed and the more important his or her perceived role). These critical mass arguments were often made by those in marketing and sales but also by other departments as well. Regardless of the legitimate reasons for growth (e.g., expansion of workload, diversification, risk mitigation, exploiting new opportunities), lower level managers could always play the critical mass card if they met resistance to their strategic or budgetary plans. Overwhelmed and inexperienced senior managers often had little basis for challenging these critical mass arguments, which seemed to make sense in a fast-growing, intensely competitive market. Against the backdrop of healthy profits with easy affordability, senior management typically approved these plans justified by critical mass arguments more out of fear of being wrong than because they represented the prudent course of action.

The addition of resources to achieve critical mass should always be challenged by senior management in order to determine whether achievement of the desired results requires the proposed increase in resources. Decisions to grow to critical mass should be more than a budgetary, affordability issue and should include a rigorous analytical process with the executive team challenging the metrics and assumptions used to determine critical mass. While critical mass in and of itself is not a bad reason to grow an organization, the business rationale behind it must be quantified, vetted, and evaluated in the context of the validity of the assumptions used, the balance sheet implications (e.g., effect on profit margins), and the long-term organizational impact. Furthermore, the hidden costs (e.g., additional support staff, facilities, training, and potential increased liabilities) associated with establishing and maintaining that critical mass and whether it is sustainable need to be understood. The benefits of these critical mass expansions must also be weighed against the increase in the complexity of managing a larger organization.

Organizational growth, including critical mass growth, becomes more challenging when companies try to maintain a high level of experience and expertise in their management and research teams. Growth in this context is particularly difficult when other companies in the same industry are seeking the same expertise and management talent. The sales force arms race, the share of voice-driven marketing budgets (i.e., the share or percentage of advertising for a particular brand in its market), and the seemingly unchecked research expansions that have occurred in many pharmaceutical companies suggest that due diligence with regard to critical mass growth over the past thirty years was driven more by affordability than considerations for the management of talent.

Mismanaging organizational growth is perhaps one of the pharmaceutical industry's biggest miscalculations over the past several decades. Unmanageable organizational size contributed to operational inefficiencies and, more importantly, to a dilution in expertise that led to reduced R&D productivity and a concurrent increase in mistakes and poor decisions. In short, the sheer size of these companies helped foster an environment that was unmanageable and counter-productive to their long-term growth and sustainability. It seems clear that given the limited availability of industry expertise and the low level of integrity exhibited over the past several decades, most pharmaceutical companies have exceeded their optimal size and are now suffering from the unintended consequences of unchecked growth.

Chapter 6
The Inherent Challenges of Large Organizations

The collapse of major U.S. banks and brokerage firms in late 2008, the bankruptcies of General Motors (resurrected with billions in government funds and now partially owned by the government) and Chrysler, and even the well-publicized problems at the FDA can all be attributed to unmanageable organizational size. Because of their sheer size, large organizations are inherently more difficult to manage effectively, and they are less likely to make needed adjustments in the face of rapidly changing market conditions. As companies grow, their risk potential increases as a result of:

- An increased need for expertise and competence;
- Broadly dispersed responsibilities and lack of accountability;
- Less diligent management oversight;
- Superficial, routine strategic and operational planning;
- Misalignment with organizational goals and objectives;
- Declining operational efficiencies;
- Bloated budgets with wasteful spending;
- Increased vulnerability to breaches of integrity; and
- More mistakes and poor decisions.

Companies face additional challenges as they grow in size. Organizational growth means larger infrastructures and more of everything—more people, products, facilities, and locations. Simply put, adding more of one thing often leads to a need for more of something else. For example, business expansion leads to a need for more people, which means more recruiting, training, office space, and office equipment. Expansion of operations to produce more products requires more manufacturing facilities, more equipment to purchase and maintain, more complex supply chains to manage, more customers to satisfy, and potentially more exposure to product liability lawsuits. Large multinational businesses have the added complexities of foreign legal compliance, language requirements, import and export challenges, and more regulatory hurdles to overcome, all of which require additional expertise, facilities, and support personnel. In larger companies, further challenges arise, including managing organizational talent development, ensuring functional accountability, staying connected with customers, planning increasingly complex strategic and operational programs, maintaining organizational alignment with the business plan, and creating an environment that is conducive to effective organizational communication both up and down the hierarchy. Missteps in any of these areas can expose the company to serious financial, legal, and regulatory consequences.

The quality (expertise, competence, and integrity) of the available talent pool is the foundation upon which a company's organizational competence and proficiency are based. As companies grow, maintaining high standards in these areas becomes increasingly difficult. While it may not be all that difficult to locate and hire five or ten people who meet the required standards, finding thousands is considerably more challenging. Companies that employ thousands or tens of thousands of individuals with functional or industry expertise can quickly deplete the pool of viable candidates, especially if other companies in the industry are seeking the same individuals. Although there may be a plethora of good candidates, the challenge is to find those people who meet or exceed the desired level of functional and industry expertise and competence. Finding candidates whose integrity is beyond reproach can further narrow the candidate pool.

Aside from the strength of the product line and the size of the market opportunity, the overall quality of the employee base is the single most important variable in determining the optimal size of a company. Employees who make good decisions and know how to get things done spend considerably less time completing important tasks than those who are inexperienced or technically unprepared. Those employees who have expertise, who are competent, and who have integrity also are less likely to make the mistakes and poor decisions that compromise a company's bottom line as well as its credibility.

In larger organizations, the likelihood that mistakes and poor decisions will occur is greater because of the larger number of people involved and decisions that are made on a daily basis. Companies and their managements tend to rely on policies highlighted in employee handbooks, training manuals, standard operating procedures, and authorization sign-offs to help reduce operational mistakes. Despite the use of these prescriptive procedures, however, large organizations are subject to system failures if the people overseeing an operation or signing off on a decision or action are not competent, have insufficient expertise, shun their managerial oversight responsibilities, or lack integrity.

Company executives play a crucial role in setting organizational expectations and providing diligent management oversight. Strong, competent management must be able to provide effective leadership, set organizational goals and objectives, effectively manage the operations to deliver on those expectations, and provide insightful feedback on progress toward reaching those goals. In addition, management must set the tone as to what will and (even more importantly) will not be tolerated while maintaining fiscal responsibility and striving to improve customer satisfaction. Needless to say, employees thrive and are generally more productive in companies with experienced leadership and good management.

As organizations grow, the challenges with regard to planning, operational oversight, budgetary and expense accountability, and customer satisfaction become extremely time-consuming. In large publicly-owned companies, investor and employee relations, administrative duties, and meetings consume an inordinate amount of time, even for competent managers. Without appropriate oversight (i.e., a lack of timely and insightful feedback), accountability diminishes, leading to organizational dysfunction and, in many cases, employee frustration and apathy. The ability to "inspect what you expect" diminishes with organizational size and, along with it, the opportunity to monitor and reinforce cultural expectations including personal and corporate integrity.

As day-to-day tasks mount in larger organizations, the strategic planning process—a critical area—begins to receive less attention. This task is often delegated to a team of business majors and financial modelers which, the executive team assumes, has rigorously vetted the assumptions and analytics of the plan in previous reviews with lower level managers. In many large organizations, strategic and budget (spending level) planning is a continuous cycle of drafting, preparing, reviewing, and presenting. The larger the company, the more supportive documentation available and the greater the volume of materials compiled for review. As a result, busy executives tend to get the distilled versions of planning presentations, which are often limited to the important conclusions with their top- and bottom-line financial implications. The assumptions underlying the process and their non-financial implications are often masked by the volume of detail, the depth of market analysis, the complexity of the business models, and the biases of lower level managers. Despite the amount of time and resources required to create these presentations, they are typically so large that comparisons with historical revenue and spending information often establish the basis for approval. With little more than a cursory review of how things look compared to previous years, busy senior managers find little perceived value in digging deep to uncover inefficiencies, wasteful spending, or outdated, obsolete business operations. Headcount, the number of employees, is always a leading topic of discussion related to controlling expenses but is rarely debated in the context of the need for expertise or personnel development planning. Unfortunately, the most senior executives, including those at the C-level (e.g., CEO, CFO, COO), often receive only condensed versions of the strategic plan in the form of slide presentations, executive summaries, and budgets that are transformed into corporate financial reports. The objective for lower level management and its teams becomes selling the plan in order to justify the proposed budget (i.e., level of spending) along with the corresponding goals and objectives.

Ironically, there seems to be an inverse relationship between the size of the organization and the ability of executives to carry out an in-depth review of the contents, rationale, assumptions, supportive data, and recommendations that are part of the strategic and operational planning process. A preoccupation with investor relations, Board of Directors activities (e.g., regular communication and meeting preparation), industry commitments, and massive amounts of information to review all lower the probability of in-depth executive due diligence in larger organizations. Exploration of strategic options and alternative decisions at the executive level becomes less rigorous as companies grow. Exceptions occur when companies find themselves in the midst of a crisis or face a challenging financial quarter or year. Even then, however, the discussions focus more on fixing the problem and controlling expenses than on formulating strategy.

Even if senior management commits to a diligent review, few executives in larger companies are close enough to their products and services, their customers, or the market to serve as a credible source of insightful commentary regarding strategic and operational plans and budgets. Executives at large companies tend to better understand the financial markets and have closer relationships with Wall Street analysts than with their customers or even their employees. Much of the information that executive management receives about customers and the market comes from reading summaries of marketing or strategic planning presentations, preparing for quarterly earnings calls with investors, or making investor relations presentations. This isolation from the market makes it more difficult for executive management to provide meaningful interpretations of the data, ask the critical questions, and assess the practicality and long-term implications of various strategic options. Over time, these limitations can lead to poor strategic decisions, bloated budgets, wasteful spending, commercialization missteps, and, even more importantly, missed opportunities to correct problems before they produce substantial negative effects on the company.

Once the strategic plans are approved and ready for execution, large organizations face the challenge of aligning expectations throughout the company. This is accomplished primarily through corporate communications programs including internal websites, quarterly teleconferences, and cameo visits by executives to various locations. Some large companies depend on trickle-down presentations, with each manager presenting to his or her own team. This approach, however, only increases the chance for misrepresentation, miscommunication, and misinterpretation over the course of hundreds of presentations to tens of thousands of employees in locations around the world.

In smaller companies, everyone (including receptionists and housekeeping staff) is brought together for presentation and discussion of the plan and management's expectations. Corporate alignment is also easier in smaller companies because a larger percentage of the organization has already been involved in the planning process. It is not that difficult to bring together a couple of hundred or a couple of thousand people once a quarter or even weekly, if necessary. Bringing together tens of thousands of employees, however, who may be located at offices throughout the world, is logistically much more challenging, particularly when multiple languages and vastly different time zones are involved. Despite the number and array of electronic communication technologies that are currently available, it is still more difficult for large companies to maintain a high level of effective, personally engaging communication with their employees. Now think about how hard it is for an employee to raise an issue or a concern with anyone beyond his or her immediate supervisor.

Managers in large corporations also find it more challenging to provide diligent operational oversight that can reinforce expected behavior, establish accountability, and avert mistakes and poor decisions with timely interventions. This sort of oversight is critical for ensuring that expectations are understood and are being met, productivity is optimized, expenses are managed appropriately, and employee morale is enhanced. It also provides an opportunity for managers to inspire creativity, share their own expertise on difficult projects, and provide career development mentoring. The lack of diligent management oversight leads to a gradual reduction in operational performance, wasteful spending, abuses in expense reporting, and unchecked mistakes and poor decisions. More importantly, poor management oversight can dampen employee morale, project an attitude of management indifference regarding performance, and undermine behavior expectations, all of which can foster an environment which unintentionally encourages breaches in personal integrity.

Executives and managers in smaller organizations realize that their limited capitalization and modest (if any) cash flows afford less room for operational inefficiencies. They also have fewer layers of management, making operational performance and the lines of accountability more apparent to higher levels in the organization. The highest ranking executives in smaller companies are usually much closer to day-to-day operations than their counterparts in larger organizations. They tend to be more aware of the appropriateness of performance expectations (i.e., whether they are realistic and achievable), the opportunities for improvement, and the expertise and competence of the employee base (having the right people in the right jobs). This transparency makes it much easier to identify and correct mistakes and poor decisions in a timely fashion. Senior executives in larger organizations, however, depend more on formal management reviews and organizational "bubbling up" (i.e., from subordinates to managers and then up the hierarchy) of information to know what is going on at operational levels. In fact, one could argue that some of the corporate missteps discussed in previous chapters occurred because of the lag time between their occurrence and their discovery by senior management. A sage manager once told me that "the only thing worse than bad news is getting bad news late." Other missteps can occur inadvertently when managers rely on inaccurate, misleading, or incorrect information to make decisions. Disconnection from operational day-to-day activities means managers must rely on information given to them by their subordinates. When expertise, competence, and integrity are lacking in the workforce, this information may be inadequate or incorrect.

Without effective management oversight, the failure to effectively transmit performance expectations and provide credible feedback to employees can also reduce productivity and dampen morale. In larger companies, most employees receive feedback from their immediate supervisors or peers. Rarely will an employee be recognized for his or her efforts by someone who is more than two levels higher up in the organization. In larger organizations, management that is two levels above an employee is unlikely to even know that person, much less care about what he or she is working on.

Larger companies also have more challenges with regard to expense management. Employees in larger companies tend to believe that there is plenty of cash to cover relatively small expense discrepancies and that management considers such matters not worth pursuing. Smaller companies, due to their limited capitalization and modest cash flows, tend to manage expenses much more carefully, with senior executives often challenging the appropriateness and the necessity of even the smallest purchases. Creating a culture of responsible expense management can dramatically improve profitability and, more importantly, make more funds available for critical projects and programs that might otherwise remain underfunded. Conversely, a lack of expense oversight can lead to wasteful spending, inflated costs, progressively more bloated budgets, and an unnecessary reduction in profitability. In larger companies, critical, frequent, and specific expense reviews can also reinforce expectations for accountability, honesty, and integrity.

The size of a company also affects its ability to make strategic and operational changes quickly. Inept or sluggish change management can be a death sentence for companies in a rapidly evolving technology-based industry. For example, by the time the U.S. automobile industry finally understood the critical importance of flexibility and adaptability to changing market conditions, it was already too late. Large organizations have massive infrastructures, too many established and difficult-to-change policies and procedures, and obsolete expertise, all of which interfere with flexibility and adaptability. Management may also be reluctant to make seemingly dramatic, high-risk strategic or tactical changes that could raise investor concerns or compromise their personal job security, careers, or opportunities for bonuses. Even if senior management does make a decision to move in another direction, the sheer inertia of large organizations means that any changes will take more time to execute than they would in smaller organizations. In the next chapter, we will discuss ways companies can grow while mitigating the risks associated with organizational growth.

Chapter 7

Critical Factors for Success in Large, Fast-Growing Organizations

Pharmaceutical companies tend to be large, fast-growing, complex organizations. As discussed earlier, their sheer size makes them difficult to manage efficiently and effectively. Many of the missteps that have occurred in the pharmaceutical industry can be attributed to the challenges of running such large corporations. Five elements are critical to the success of these firms. While other business factors are also important (e.g., marketing products that customers actually need and then pricing them appropriately), the following factors are particularly relevant to fast-growing pharmaceutical companies: leadership; expertise and competence; integrity; clearly defined roles, responsibilities, and expectations; and diligent management oversight.

Leadership

The concept of leadership has been explored in countless books, seminars, publications, and websites. Most industry executives have participated in more than their share of leadership programs and have read the latest books on the subject, all of which suggest that leadership is critical to the success of any organization. It would be easy to blame the pharmaceutical industry's current dysfunctional state solely on a lack of leadership. Clearly, both past and present pharmaceutical company executives deserve a good deal of criticism for not addressing the issues that confront the industry or providing the vision, guidance, and bold strategic interventions to address those issues. Ongoing concerns regarding integrity, organizational priorities, and corporate mismanagement all suggest a desperate need for stronger leadership throughout the industry. Indeed, strong leadership could (and should) have prevented many of the organizational missteps that have already come to light. Strong leaders must have the courage to make difficult decisions, to intervene when necessary, and to change course when the status quo is no longer the best option. An exclusive focus on leadership, however, can obscure the underlying factors that contributed to the poor decisions made by pharmaceutical industry executives in the past. Despite having its share of good leaders, the pharmaceutical industry has demonstrated that management that lacks expertise, competence, and integrity has limited value and carries the potential to produce severe negative consequences.

Although strong leadership is essential for effective management, eventually all fast-growing companies reach a point at which their size exceeds the capacity of their leadership to be effective. At this point, the positive impact of leadership diminishes, strategic vision becomes less clear, corporate culture gets distorted, inspiration is diluted or lost, and employees feel disconnected and unappreciated. This disconnect from employees and customers has been highlighted in the reality television show "Undercover Boss" in which C-level executives disguise themselves as rank-and-file workers to allow them to participate in the experiences of ordinary employees in their own companies. It wasn't until after they left their corporate suites that these executives gained an appreciation for the work their employees were doing and how some of the bureaucratically imposed corporate processes and procedures were negatively affecting productivity and morale. The key take-away message is that even in larger organizations, executives need to stay connected with their employees and customers. Strong effective leadership coupled with expertise, competence, and integrity are essential for organizational growth and can significantly increase a company's chances for long-term success.

Expertise and competence

Expertise can be defined as a combination of knowledge and experience. Competence is the ability to perform a task consistently well, and proficiency is usually attained through repetitive execution of a task. Knowledge can be acquired formally through academic studies and/or self-study. The knowledge component of expertise is not some predetermined level of comprehension but rather an ongoing effort to maintain a deep appreciation of a particular field of interest or of its principles. For scientists, the knowledge component of expertise may lie in a particular area of research; for managers, it may mean keeping up with strategic or tactical developments in their functional areas of responsibilities, and for executives it implies staying current with corporate governance, regulatory and legal issues, and economic trends that affect the industry. The knowledge component of expertise is the didactic informational foundation for job performance and decision-making.

As in any profession, levels of expertise and competence vary greatly across the spectrum of available talent. In a payer-valued market, those with the highest perceived level of expertise and competence are financially rewarded to a greater extent than those with less expertise and competence. A corollary to this observation is that a higher level of performance is expected from those with the highest expertise and competence. Unfortunately, at least from a societal perspective, the number of individuals who possess true expertise and competence is limited. The explosive growth of pharmaceutical companies over the past few decades suggests that this fact has not been well understood by managers at these organizations, despite the fact that establishing and maintaining high levels of expertise and competence can produce a tremendous competitive advantage. This concept is illustrated by professional sports leagues whose owners understand the value created by limiting both the number of teams in their leagues and the number of players allowed on each team.

Expertise is generally not transferable; true expertise requires in-depth knowledge that is supported by relevant real-world applications and personal experiences. Reading a book on cell-based assays does not mean that you know how to create or build cell-based assays or apply them to research or that you have any level of expertise in the field. Even inherently talented people require a certain amount of experience to establish and maintain a credible level of expertise and competence. Also, knowledge without experience and its converse—experience without knowledge (repetitive routine work with no acquisition of new knowledge)—are both of limited value. Examples of the former can be found in companies that mistake academic credentials for expertise and hire MBAs right out of top business schools to do marketing planning for products in an industry in which they have no experience, or in companies that recruit medical school professors to manage drug development. While over time these tactics can significantly increase the expertise in a company, the fact remains that most pharmaceutical company executives have unrealistic, industry-specific, near-term performance expectations (e.g., blockbuster product launches, faster drug development, etc.) that exceed the experience base of these academic types.

Deficiencies in pharmaceutical industry expertise vary and can be functional, technical, legal, regulatory, or even market- or patient-nuanced. Some support staff functions, including a few administrative and technician positions, require limited industry-specific expertise. There are few exceptions, however, to the need for relevant industry expertise within a pharmaceutical company. Employees with expertise and competence are able to understand the context and circumstances in which they operate and will perform tasks at a higher level of proficiency with a higher probability of success than those who do not have the requisite background. Even more importantly, these employees are more likely to sort through decision-making options and better analyze the implications of various possible outcomes before initiating any actions.

Individuals who posses the knowledge base and experience to understand the nuances of a particular job also have enhanced organizational credibility (i.e., the belief that a person knows what he/she is talking about). Other than managers who are directly involved in the matter, these people are often the only ones who can prevent poor decisions from being acted upon. This is especially true when the message is organizationally difficult to accept, such as when the results of a trial are not as good as expected, forecasts already approved are in error, or a particular strategy that had previously been favored is found to be flawed. In companies that are expertise-deficient (and even in some that are not), incompetent people who are articulate, who look professional, and who know how to play the game (or who ride the coattails of a more senior person who is considered a rising star) can acquire undeserved organizational credibility. If management also lacks expertise, the mistakes and poor decisions made by these incompetent people may go unrecognized and unchecked. Although most pharmaceutical companies can tolerate and absorb a modest number of mistakes and poor decisions, when their number and magnitude exceed the ability of management to provide adequate oversight and timely interventions, companies become unduly exposed to regulatory, legal, financial, and other business vulnerabilities.

Many pharmaceutical companies, in part due to insatiable demands for growth, promoted seemingly knowledgeable competent employees to more senior positions before these individuals had a chance to acquire a strong foundational experience base. Companies typically underestimated or ignored the value of keeping people in positions for a reasonable period of time to allow them to experience the consequences of their decision-making. Employees who advanced rapidly also missed the opportunity to broaden their knowledge, sharpen their skills, and develop a stronger industry-related context of the business. Even the best commercial and research professionals in the industry have struggled to develop the necessary expertise given the abbreviated timeframes spent in development positions. These timeframes were shortened further when start-up biotech companies began hiring researchers and managers from the pharmaceutical industry, many of whom were attracted by innovative new technologies and large stock-option grants with promising upside potential. This competition for talent between pharmaceutical companies and start-up biotech firms led to a further dilution in expertise across the industry.

As the pharmaceutical industry struggled to keep up with the growing complexities of the market, management and research expertise became diluted, especially at senior levels in the industry. The large number of new products introduced during the past three to four decades and the growing need for management forced companies to promote (often based on political savvy or likeability) marketing, sales, and research personnel into positions of increased responsibility before they were ready. In these boom times for the industry, career advancement opportunities were available to all. The talent pool became increasingly diluted as more companies looking for the same expertise continued to recruit, hire, and promote.

Eventually, rapid advancement up the organizational ladder became the expected norm in the pharmaceutical industry. Ambitious employees were more interested in prestigious titles, larger offices, more perks, and bigger paychecks than in developing additional skills and expertise. In fact, over the past several decades, growth in the industry was so robust that ambitious middle-level managers who were not promoted within one or two years began to entertain other, more lucrative job prospects in the industry—opportunities that were often brought to them by industry recruiters or headhunters.

Problems due to marginal experience as a result of rapid career advancement in the industry were further compounded by the fact that those who were promoted often found themselves in positions that were beyond their expertise. Often the manager-in-training was working with subordinates who were also in training, leading to an untenable situation in which the blind were leading the blind. As a result, management oversight and the decision-making process were compromised by the limited experience of senior managers and their subordinates. For example, if someone had never participated in an exacting marketing planning process, it is unlikely that he or she would be able to provide credible, insightful criticisms or determine the validity of the assumptions and conclusions comprising a new marketing plan. Also, the task of dealing with the consequences of mistakes and poor decisions made by those who were too rapidly promoted often fell on the shoulders of the new manager. "Cleaning up somebody else's mess" became a common frustration in this rapidly growing industry.

One way for fast-growing companies to deal with the problem of insufficient numbers of employees with the necessary expertise is to create proactive development plans, particularly for those being groomed for management positions. Strategically moving key people throughout an organization for development purposes is an essential strategy for company and industry growth. However, grooming may or may not translate into job promotion. For example, good salespeople need development paths to help them become either great salespeople or managers (regardless of whether they are going to be promoted or not), and good research scientists need development paths to help them become outstanding scientists or managers (regardless of whether they are going to be promoted or not). These paths represent personal development growth opportunities for people with expertise and competence in their current jobs, which differs from being placed in an assignment to grow into that position. For those individuals who have already demonstrated expertise in their current positions, expanding one's horizons by growing into a new position is critical, especially for those seeking executive roles. The bottom line is that the appropriate management of talent (based on expertise and competence rather than political savvy or likeability) plays an important role in organizational development and succession planning.

On the other hand, when companies become so large that virtually everyone is growing into a position, there is an organizational loss of functionality, especially in rapidly growing organizations in which the learning curve is longer than the time spent in the development position. When the majority of management employees are placed into roles that are beyond their level of expertise, the organization is too large for the talent pool to support. These organizations are more prone to operational inefficiencies and the types of mistakes and poor decisions discussed in earlier chapters. While it is difficult to know whether there is less absolute expertise in the industry than in the past, it is clear that the available expertise is now spread across many more companies (both large and small) than in the 1970s and 1980s.

Integrity

Healthcare providers and their patients must be able to trust the information that pharmaceutical companies disseminate about their products. Patients must also be able to trust that the drugs being prescribed have been adequately tested in clinical trials, are safe, and are marketed with full disclosure of their potential risks and side effects. Unfortunately, this trust has been compromised by numerous breaches of individual and corporate integrity, resulting in public distrust and resentment. In far too many instances, pharmaceutical marketers employed the same sales and marketing tactics for prescription drugs as they would for any commodity and either forgot, failed to consider, or, more likely, failed to care that a patient's health and possibly his or her life might be at stake. A lack of rigorous management oversight and corrective intervention helped create an environment in which compromises in personal integrity went unchecked, leading many employees, and some managers, to feel that their indiscretions had become acceptable or even expected. A mindset consisting of the idea that "management must approve if they haven't said anything" became the norm and led to a belief in many companies that just about anything was acceptable as long as it drove sales.

Before the 1980s, pharmaceutical companies built strong cultural expectations around patient care and the importance of integrity. Employees believed they were doing something special with their careers by helping the sick, and they had an inherent understanding that the discovery of each new product meant that somebody's suffering would be alleviated. This sense of purpose was often cited as the main reason why many people wanted to work in the pharmaceutical industry. This altruistic vision also provided a strong foundation for personal and business ethics and integrity. Almost sixty years ago, the German chemist George Merck, son of the founder of Merck & Co. Inc., proclaimed that "Medicine is for the people. It is not for the profits."[1] Unfortunately, the actions and behavior of the pharmaceutical industry over the past several decades have demonstrated that the industry—including companies like Merck—has forgotten what George Merck said back in 1952. For management to knowingly approve or intentionally ignore the egregious commercial and scientific indiscretions that have been documented suggests a serious erosion of personal and corporate integrity that has been exacerbated by the arrogance of those who attempted to rationalize their unconscionable actions. With the seemingly endless examples of impropriety (which continue to this day), one has to wonder whether the industry can once again become a trusted source of safe drugs and credible information. What will it take for the industry to reorder its priorities and understand that finding treatments and cures to relieve the suffering of patients is what the pharmaceutical industry is all about—not revenue growth and stock price?

In order for pharmaceutical companies to grow and succeed, they must develop a corporate culture that supports and embraces integrity. Without it, patients and the healthcare market will continue to distrust the industry and will place constraints on long-term growth and viability. Companies that cannot be trusted to provide full and complete information about their products will have great difficulty selling their new products for true market value, regardless of how innovative they are.

Clearly defined roles and expectations

In a complex business such as pharmaceuticals, employees in large companies must have a clear understanding of the organizational structure of their company including the responsibilities associated with different job functions as well as expectations regarding their personal performance. This knowledge can significantly enhance operational efficiency, help reduce turf wars between various departmental factions (frequently referred to as "silos" in Big Pharma), and mitigate finger-pointing by highlighting clear lines of accountability when problems arise. Many company executives and managers assume that titles, departments, and job descriptions provide sufficient information to communicate organizational roles and responsibilities. Although this may be true in smaller, less complex environments, in most large pharmaceutical companies, job functions and responsibilities vary from division to division or even within the same department. For example, a product manager's job function may vary depending on the products he or she works on, how large the product team is, and how a particular marketing manager wants to organize his or her team. The concept of cross-functional teams (across departments or even across divisions) further disperses responsibilities and obscures individual accountability.

A clear set of goals and objectives can translate organizational roles and responsibilities into expectations and can help employees understand how their work contributes to the overall work product of the organization. The process of developing, setting, and maintaining goals and objectives is the job of management, which is also responsible for ensuring that goals and objectives are meaningful, that they accurately reflect corporate expectations, and that they can lead to the desired results. In smaller organizations where management is closer to daily operations, communicating expectations and assessing progress is much more of an ongoing (daily or weekly) process. The inherent complexities of larger organizations, however, make it more difficult for management to provide this oversight and feedback. The following are common mistakes that occur as a result of inexperienced personnel and/or poor management oversight:

- Setting goals and objectives that are too far removed from daily operational activities and expectations;
- Setting goals and objectives that are activity-based and not results-oriented;
- Assigning too many goals and objectives;
- Setting goals and objectives that are driven by incentive compensation expectations; and

- Infrequent monitoring including lack of feedback and timely and appropriate adjustments.

Having a meaningless or unrealistic set of goals and objectives is a frequent source of confusion and frustration for employees and is often a point of contention during year-end performance reviews and compensation discussions. For maximum effectiveness, daily operational activities and expectations should be clearly aligned with assigned goals and objectives; the latter should be high-impact (i.e., they should have a direct impact on value creation such as research pipeline progress, revenue generation, or operational efficiency) and also results-oriented.

One day during my career as a sales representative, an astute manager, sitting next to me in a meeting, wrote on a napkin that "activities do not equal results." Inexperienced managers often confuse the effort expended or the activities performed in the pursuit of assigned goals and objectives with the results they are trying to achieve. It is not uncommon to deliver the activity (e.g., ten symposia or five publications) without reaching the goal (e.g., raising target audience awareness of clinical efficacy data by 5%). Having too many goals and objectives also adds to organizational inefficiency by confusing employees about their priorities, thereby diluting their efforts. Based on this author's experience, the imposition of more than ten goals per year is beyond the reasonable work capacity of most individuals and decreases the likelihood that any of the high-impact goals will be accomplished. Furthermore, having too many goals suggests that management is focused more on activity than on results.

Setting meaningless goals and objectives is often driven by incentive compensation. It is no secret that the CEO of the company (who in many cases may also be the Chairman of the Board), on behalf of his or her management team, submits recommendations for goals and objectives to be met during the upcoming year to the Board of Directors compensation committee for review and approval. Although management must defend its proposal, it is unlikely that they would recommend goals and objectives that cannot be achieved. (Management almost always anticipates some pushback on its goal-setting proposals, so that even if adjustments are demanded by the Board, management's goals and objectives are still achievable.) Once approved, with bonus opportunities defined, these goals and objectives are then passed down the organization. Managers earn their bonuses if their subordinates achieve their goals and objectives. To keep goals relevant and meaningful, frequent management reviews should allow for adjustments (e.g., changes in strategy, priorities, or budgets) while also providing an opportunity to discuss challenges and acknowledge accomplishments. Ironically, the use of review of performance against goals and objectives tends to diminish where it is needed the most—in larger organizations. Although one might expect such reviews to be a top priority of managers whose bonuses are linked to results, in many large companies the Human Resources department is given the task of coordinating the review process at mid-year and year-end reviews to ensure that managers take the time and appropriately review performance as it pertains to goals and objectives. Not surprisingly, managers often regard performance reviews as a nuisance, interfering with their daily administrative duties and operational and problem-solving activities. In larger organizations, it is also more difficult and takes more management expertise to meaningfully align the daily activities of lower level and front-line workers with overall corporate goals and objectives, particularly if the organization includes divisions in different businesses and in foreign countries. Based on my experience, organizations that excel at setting and managing realistic and meaningful goals and objectives are operationally more efficient and consistently deliver more high-impact results. When people know what is expected of them, they can focus on delivering the results without becoming distracted by easier to achieve but less important tasks. At year's end, employees also tend to have a real sense of accomplishment, and their performance reviews tend to be less contentious. Effective goal setting and performance management are almost daily activities in smaller organizations, but they are actually more important in large organizations.

Diligent management oversight

Effective oversight is a management competency that requires both know-how and experience. Sometimes labeled "micro-management" when used to usurp autonomy, initiative, and the decision-making authority of subordinates, skillful management oversight is best done with a nurturing, coaching mindset that guides and inspires employees while allowing managers to maintain control over their areas of responsibility in the organization. Regardless of the approach employed during the oversight process, there is absolutely no justification for management to plead ignorance about decisions or activities in their areas of responsibility that could potentially jeopardize or damage the company. Simply put, if a CEO is unaware of off-label promotion, or the use of falsified scientific data to gain FDA approval or to promote a product, or inappropriate payments to healthcare providers, either the oversight process needs to be reassessed or the organization is too large to be managed effectively.

Staying abreast of what is happening in the company may involve informal discussions with employees, reading reports and computer-generated performance dashboards, attending daily operational meetings, weekly update meetings, and/or monthly reviews, and, perhaps most importantly, asking relevant and insightful questions. Each manager (and executive) should strive to achieve a complete understanding of what is going on in his or her area of responsibility and to be aware of any issues (internal, customer, or market) that could adversely affect the company. Value-added management oversight also involves intervening to mitigate risk, adjusting resources to facilitate goal achievement, providing insight on challenging projects and difficult situations, keeping teams focused on high-impact goals, and finding ways to leverage employee input on operational improvements or new research findings without distracting team members from their priorities. Even employees with high levels of expertise and competence have a need for and can benefit from frequent and competent management reviews and oversight.

As companies grow in organizational size, diligent management oversight becomes more challenging, but its benefits to the organization increase. When management oversight diminishes, it becomes less value-added while risks and challenges to the company increase. Company executives (and Boards of Directors) need to take whatever actions are necessary to ensure that the size of the organization does not preclude diligent management oversight at all levels.

In the final analysis, the manageable size of any organization is determined by the expertise, competence, and integrity of its employees, including the management team. Setting clear goals and objectives combined with diligent management oversight can mitigate risk and increase the probability of producing the desired results in large organizations.

Chapter 8
Complexity in the Pharmaceutical Industry

Rapid advances in science and medicine, the simultaneous evolution of healthcare market dynamics, and progressively more restrictive regulatory and legal constraints have created an increasingly complex business environment for the pharmaceutical industry. This increasing complexity may constitute one of the biggest challenges the industry has ever faced, and one that will likely persist well into the future. Although many businesses struggle with some degree of complexity, the pharmaceutical industry has multiple layers of complexity in virtually every aspect of its business. In later chapters we will delve into more detail regarding some of the functional complexities (e.g., sales and marketing, research, executive management) in the industry and provide examples of how missteps in these areas have had very negative consequences. In this chapter we will discuss five major sources of complexity for the industry: rapid advances in science, medicine, and technology; ever-changing healthcare market dynamics; increasing regulatory and legal considerations; management of complex interrelationships; and increasing organizational size.

Rapid advances in science, medicine, and technology

Increasing complexity in the pharmaceutical industry is best manifested by its need to stay current with rapid advances in science, medicine, and technology. Despite incredible accomplishments in molecular biology including the decoding of the human genome and new technologies for studying genomics and proteomics, we have yet to turn this information into the highly anticipated stream of innovative new drug treatments. Nevertheless, the search for new therapeutic agents is now being driven by elaborate and sophisticated research technologies (cell-based assays, gene sequencers, mass spectrometers, and non-invasive remote cardiac monitors). Rapid scientific progress is occurring even in research areas from which the apparent targets of diseases have already been mined. For example, G-protein-coupled receptors, which comprise a large family of transmembrane receptors that activate signal transduction pathways inside the cell, are the target for as many as 40% of all prescription drugs on the market, but this family continues to be explored for additional mechanisms and sites of interaction for yet to be identified therapeutic agents.[1]

The industry is now so specialized that highly trained scientific and technical personnel are required at every stage of drug discovery, development, commercialization, and manufacturing. It is not uncommon to find people with advanced degrees in the life sciences, including pharmacists and nurses, in the ranks of sales, marketing, and operations management. Similarly, Quality Control and Quality Assurance departments, for example, often employ as many scientists, statisticians, and laboratory technicians as does R&D.

Pharmaceutical companies monetize their discovery efforts through patents (intellectual property rights). Corporate patent attorneys (often with graduate degrees in the life sciences) help scientists translate laboratory notebook entries into patent filings that explicitly describe the scientific and technical details of discoveries. Patents affect virtually every aspect of the industry, from the research tools it uses to discover new drugs to the chemistry of the products it develops and the formulations it uses to deliver drugs to the target site in the proper concentrations. Even manufacturing processes themselves are affected by patents. Intellectual property represents the foundation of any proprietary pharmaceutical company, and a strong contemporary patent portfolio is essential for long-term success.

Quite simply, patents formalize the practical applications of advances in science and technology. They also add to the complexity of the industry, primarily because multidisciplinary discoveries are often not exclusive to a particular company or even to the pharmaceutical industry. Virtually thousands of researchers, physicians, and other healthcare professionals and scientists in government, the military, medical schools, academia, private practice, as well as other industries (e.g., the chemical, food, and cosmetics industries) have undertaken and continue to pursue research projects relevant to the pharmaceutical industry, and these projects often yield findings that have the potential to be patented. Therefore, in addition to employees of other pharmaceutical companies, non-industry scientists have the opportunity to make discoveries, develop intellectual property, and file patents that can either assist (by licensing access to intellectual property) or thwart a pharmaceutical company's efforts to develop, manufacture, and commercialize new drugs. If licensing or partnering negotiations fail, such patents can compromise a company's drug development program and dampen commercial interest in pursuing a potentially valuable treatment.

While a discussion of information technology (computers, software, data storage, and electronic sharing) is beyond the scope of this book, suffice it to say that computers and the ability to store, retrieve, analyze, and share large volumes of data have greatly facilitated advances in science and medicine. Today, virtually all laboratory instrumentation and data generation processes are electronic and computer assisted. Computer technology has also raised the bar as to what should be possible (e.g., decoding the human genome, complex multi-study meta-analysis, and computational drug design). In fact, much of the drug discovery and development work being done today would simply not be possible without the information technologies currently in use. Ironically, while computer technology has contributed to the increasing complexity of the pharmaceutical industry, it has also become an indispensable tool for managing the business.

Ever-changing healthcare market dynamics

Once the FDA approves a new drug for marketing, the complexities of the healthcare market itself come into play. Although launching a new drug has always involved the use of significant resources for strategic marketing, product positioning, marketing communications, and physician targeting, the fact is that commercialization in the 1970s and 1980s was much less complicated than it is today. It involved training sales representatives so that they were proficient in delivering an effective presentation to a small group of targeted physicians (identified as high-volume prescribers), sponsoring continuing medical education programs, exhibiting at appropriate medical meetings and conferences, and having effective advertising in the right medical journals. In those days, there were few concerns about the cost of therapy because treatment options were limited to only a few competitive products, and "managed care" referred to the Veterans Administration and medical center hospital formularies.

This rather straightforward but simplistic approach to marketing new drugs did not last long. The increasing complexity of commercialization resulting from marketing a relatively large number of less differentiated products in a progressively more managed healthcare market is best exemplified by the complex web of influencers (local and national opinion leaders) and tiers of decision-makers who now decide which drugs are available at what level of reimbursement to which patients. While the market as well as patients may still believe that physicians have the final say in determining what products to prescribe for their patients, the fact is that physicians are significantly influenced and in many cases, restricted, in their drug product choices by government and private insurance plans attempting to reduce or control the cost of drug treatment. In addition, some pharmacies have been given financial incentives by health insurance plans and their Pharmacy Benefits Managers to encourage physicians to switch one branded product for another or to substitute generic drugs for branded products, thus further interfering with physician choice.

The numbers and types of personnel and institutions that influence prescribing have increased dramatically over the past several decades, making it increasingly difficult to determine how to effectively market and sell pharmaceuticals. Physicians may simply have a pre-approved list of formulary drugs they can prescribe or they may be required to call a toll-free number to obtain prior approval from an insurance company to prescribe a specific drug brand. To further complicate matters, physicians have patients who are covered by many different prescription drug plans, each with its own formularies and restrictions and varying levels of reimbursement and patient co-pay requirements. Determining who actually influences prescribing, where they are located, and what information they require to support the use of products has become extremely difficult, posing commercialization challenges for even the most sophisticated marketing teams.

In addition to these challenges, the pharmaceutical industry is about to take on another level of market complexity. The recent passage of healthcare reform will mean that millions of previously uninsured Americans will now be able to obtain health insurance and prescription drug coverage. Healthcare reform, however, will require an intensified effort to control rising costs. Payers will have to be more selective about what they include on their formularies and provide incentives to encourage even greater use of generic drugs. Some form of direct or indirect controls on the cost of prescription drugs will likely be instituted such as aggressive rebate (discount) expectations, the legalization of drug reimportation (i.e., bringing cheaper drugs into the United States from other countries), and even direct negotiation of drug prices with the government. In summary, despite some initial upside for the industry from healthcare reform, it seems clear that market forces will mandate a comprehensive reevaluation of pharmaceutical pricing and commercialization strategies to address the concerns of an increasingly cost-conscious managed market.

Increasing regulatory and legal considerations

Considering that the health and safety of millions of Americans are at stake, it is not surprising that the pharmaceutical industry is one of the most regulated in existence today. Regulatory complexities and advances in science and technology continue to affect virtually every aspect of the industry. From research to manufacturing and commercialization, the FDA and their foreign counterparts regulate almost everything the industry does with the exception of finance (which is regulated by the Securities and Exchange Commission). Even information technology (e.g., the need for validated systems) and human resources (e.g., the employment of qualified personnel and compliance with the FDA's list of debarred individuals) are affected by regulation.

Perhaps one of the most challenging regulatory problems is the inability of the FDA to provide clear guidance to pharmaceutical companies as they apply advances in science, medicine, and technology. For example, the FDA has not provided meaningful instructions on how the industry can use the Internet and social media for advertising and promotion. One consequence of this lack of direction is that companies receive warning letters from the FDA about the use of these new communications tools. The industry is thus in the difficult position of trying to interpret and apply traditional FDA compliance standards to evolving new technologies. Readers should think about the difficulty of complying with the regulatory requirement to provide fair balanced product information (often in the form of a brief summary or full package insert) in a tweet on Twitter when the sender is limited to 140 characters or less or a search result for a product-related website. Or the problems involved in tracking, assessing, and following up on the validity of adverse reaction comments or inaccurate information posted on the Internet.

The FDA regulatory approval process for new drugs and biologics has also become more challenging and complex. Changes in administrations and regulatory personnel over the course of a drug's development plus confusing, sometimes contradictory, and outdated guidance documents often leave drug developers in the difficult position of having to guess what the FDA will require years later when a drug comes up for approval. Similarly, regulatory trial design expectations are making it extremely difficult to find qualified and willing patient populations that are large enough to meet the statistical requirements to establish definitive efficacy and safety. Even more frustrating are changes in trial design requirements and expectations after thousands of patients have already been enrolled and treated in a clinical trial, thus requiring a new set of clinical trials to conform to the new requirements. Drug development teams must also try to anticipate what an independent FDA advisory board of experts will deem "satisfactory results" when it meets to consider approval based on its review, interpretation, and discussion of clinical trial data summaries.

Regulatory issues are closely related to the legal complexities that are an inherent part of the industry. If the regulatory requirements on a particular matter are unclear or insufficient, it is almost certain that a legal consideration will preclude an action under consideration or at least introduce another element that must be considered before taking action. Legislation has now been enacted that bans many previously accepted business practices that involved providing healthcare professionals with perks and privileges. In an effort to mitigate pharmaceutical company influence on prescribing practices, any gift or gesture that directly or indirectly benefits the physician or his or her practice is now restricted or banned outright. In fact, many normal business practices (e.g., meals, golf outings, etc.) that were commonly used for relationship building in the past are now strictly prohibited.

Some of these legislative actions represent well-deserved punishments for the industry's abuses and unacceptable behaviors discussed in previous chapters. *Some* of the litigation, however, is due to the complexity of (or the inability of companies to stay current with) state and federal requirements, changes in regulatory enforcement practices for marketing and sales activity, or miscalculation or inaccurate reporting of pricing information. Laws and regulations may seem clear in their intent, but their practical application in the marketplace often leads to situational ambiguity (e.g., was it an educational grant or a bribe?), regional compliance uncertainty (e.g., in which states does this particular requirement apply?), and alternative interpretations (e.g., do we include samples in this discount calculation?). Once focused on providing effective, accurate, and regulatory compliant advertising and promotion that offered fair balance (equal information on safety and efficacy), pharmaceutical marketers must now comply with extensive federal, state, and country-specific legal interpretations of what they can and cannot do in the marketplace. Given the excesses and indiscretions of the past, it is doubtful that anyone is shedding tears for the pharmaceutical industry. Indeed, these market-imposed complexities are intentionally challenging and designed to eliminate, discourage, and control some of the more objectionable activities of the past.

Management of complex interrelationships

Complexity in the pharmaceutical industry has created a web of interrelationships that mandate a cautious approach to decision-making. Inexperience and situational ignorance (not knowing what to do in a particular circumstance) can often cause problems when people do not understand the organizational, legal, or regulatory implications of a decision or particular course of action. Taking advantage of an opportunity or mitigating the effects of one problem often leads to the creation of another problem, perhaps in another department or even another division of the company. We have already alluded to the pervasive effects of patents, especially the effects of an as yet undisclosed patent, on the drug discovery process. While a company may be on solid ground with regard to a patent on a specific compound, this may not be true for the manufacturing process for that compound. Knowingly (or even unknowingly) proceeding with a project that has infringement potential can be disastrous, resulting in the waste of millions of dollars in development costs or possibly even treble damages from a lost infringement suit over a marketed product. Another example of this interrelated complexity occurs when sales or marketing people attempt to satisfy a healthcare provider's (e.g., a managed care organization or hospital system) demand for pricing concessions and discounts, which may make sense from a commercial standpoint but which may conflict with the government's "best price" rule* or may be illegal for any number of other reasons (e.g., it could be considered a bribe or kickback depending on how it was paid and to whom). Still another example of this interrelated complexity might involve setting an extraordinarily high price for a newly launched product that results in negative formulary and reimbursement decisions for the company's entire product line. These are just a few examples of the complex web of interrelationships that exist in the pharmaceutical industry that can create unexpected or unintended problems and missteps for companies and individuals. It takes industry experience and expertise to avoid the pitfalls generated by these interrelated, multifunctional complexities.

Increasing organizational size

The industry's response to these complexities has been to add more resources to keep up with advances in science, technology, and medicine in an effort to meet the expectations of an increasingly demanding market and to comply with increasingly restrictive legal and regulatory requirements. As was discussed in a previous chapter, managing large complex organizations that are already laboring under the need for increased research productivity against a backdrop of intensifying regulatory, legal, and commercialization challenges adds significant operational complexity to these companies. And while most pharmaceutical companies are already multinational to some extent, the pursuit of further growth through global expansion has recently become a higher organizational priority for many of them. As attractive as this strategy may be, at its most basic level, global expansion adds yet another dimension of complexity to pharmaceutical companies.

* Many federal government contracts (i.e., Federal Supply Schedule for prescription drugs) require contractors to provide the government with products and services at the best price available to any customer. Failure to do so may be considered fraud and violates the False Claims Act.

As we have seen, the inherent complexities of the pharmaceutical industry raise serious questions about the practicalities of running large complex organizations. In the next few chapters, we will discuss how pharmaceutical companies evolved in this increasingly complex environment and how diminished expertise and poor management oversight led to reduced R&D productivity, aggressive and over-the-top marketing and sales activities, and compromises in personal, scientific, and corporate integrity that ultimately provoked public distrust and resentment of the entire industry.

Chapter 9

The Pharmaceutical Sales Representative: An Endangered Species

Expertise in pharmaceutical commercialization (i.e., marketing and sales) is often underappreciated, even by those in the industry. By assuming that competence is transferable from other industries or easily acquired in college, graduate school, or on the job, many companies and executives in the industry began to take commercialization expertise for granted as they rapidly grew their organizations over the past twenty-five years. A major premise of this book is that rapid growth led to diminished expertise and competence, which in turn significantly weakened the ability of individuals and companies to avoid mistakes and poor decisions involving aggressive and, at times, illegal sales and marketing tactics that ultimately led to increased litigation and regulation of the industry.

Before the massive corporate expansions of the past few decades, the development of pharmaceutical industry expertise often began with a sales position (as a sales representative or "rep," or as it was known historically, as a drug company detail man). Experience as a sales representative provided the individual with a foundation for understanding the market and the pharmaceutical commercialization process. As one of the most frequent entry points into the pharmaceutical industry, these jobs were usually reserved for college graduates with life-science backgrounds, especially nurses and pharmacists. The jobs were difficult to obtain, and there was considerable competition for them at major companies like Eli Lilly, Upjohn (which merged with Pharmacia in 1995), Merck, and Lederle (acquired by Wyeth in 1994). Rigorous training, high work ethic standards, challenging medical discussions with physicians, and accountability (a quaint concept today) made it just as difficult to remain employed for those not willing to make the commitment. These technically demanding jobs required ongoing product and therapeutic area training (often done on one's own time). Sales representatives also spent as many hours with their district sales managers, whose job was to coach and mentor those reps who reported to them. Frequent corporate meetings and seminars ensured that sales people stayed current but also added to the time commitment required of each of them. Indeed, it was not uncommon for sales personnel to find their lives centering on the activities of the company. While these jobs were challenging, they were also satisfying from a professional standpoint, with financial security, excellent healthcare benefits, and seemingly endless potential for personal and career development. At the same time, an unspoken but mutually beneficial paternalistic contract stated in effect: "Work hard for us and we'll take care of you. And if you can't meet our standards and performance expectations, we'll find somebody who can."

Even during the expansions of pharmaceutical sales forces in the early 1980s, the selection process was intense and competitive despite the relatively large number of new positions available (perhaps a couple of thousand at any one time). It was not uncommon for a candidate to undergo screening interviews for a full day with five or more district sales managers, senior sales representatives, and human resources personnel. A candidate may have been asked to return for a second or even third round of interviews once the initial screening process was complete. Although the sales position was the immediate need, development potential was also being assessed to determine whether the candidate had management capabilities or skills that could be applied elsewhere in the organization at some point in the future. While the district sales manager made the final decision on hiring, the other managers who had conducted interviews provided plenty of feedback. Offers to join the company were understood to be contingent on the successful completion of an initial sales training program.

Getting hired was just the beginning. Initial sales training was challenging and time consuming. Sales reps had to pass weeks of standardized training and testing; those who lacked a strong work ethic rarely made it through this initial training experience. The training was conducted by a staff of experienced full-time career trainers who were supported by more seasoned senior sales representatives and district sales managers who were being evaluated and groomed for positions of greater responsibility in the company. Trainers were held accountable for the competence of new sales reps in the field as assessed by district sales managers' reports. Trainers who gave passing marks to those who were not ready to function effectively in the field risked having their credibility called into question.

The science and product training required of sales reps was often as challenging as any advanced biology or chemistry classes taken in college. New reps were expected to become knowledgeable about a particular disease, how the disease was treated, the role of their product in the treatment of the disease, and how their product compared to other treatment options. In most companies, sales reps were responsible for multiple therapeutic areas, which required a fairly broad understanding of science and medicine.

Tests were designed to make sure that reps had a sufficient depth of knowledge of a disease to confidently and accurately hold an intelligent discussion with a physician. If a rep could not pass the tests (usually with a score of 90% or better), there was a good chance that he (in the 1970s and 1980s most sales reps were men) would be asked to resign from the company. In addition to tests of facts, training also included oral presentations to ensure that reps were fluent in disease management and medical terminology. Reps were also assessed for general professionalism (e.g., in dress, in interactions with others, and in establishing rapport). Training also included instruction in business-related matters (e.g., how to read a financial report, what is and is not an acceptable business expense, how to fill out an expense and weekly activity report) and role playing to help sales reps develop the appropriate responses to various situations that might occur in the field.

After a sales rep mastered the basic science behind a specific disease, he or she was expected to essentially memorize the package insert and become accomplished at product presentations. Trainers emphasized that physicians will "test your knowledge" and that it would be embarrassing not to know the answer to a question about the company's product, especially if the answer was in the package insert. At the same time, because interactions with physicians were expected to be friendly and open, presentations were often conversational in tone rather than memorized or "canned." Sounding like you were simply regurgitating the company line was (and still is) one of the best ways to diminish one's credibility with physicians.

Understanding the diagnostic and therapeutic challenges that physicians faced in their practices was as important as understanding the science behind a disease. Reps recognized and understood and appreciated the importance of discussions about possible adverse reactions and side effects, which were not considered competitive disadvantages but rather important facts for physicians to know and share with their patients. Not all patients were good candidates for a particular product, and reps helped physicians understand who was a good candidate and what to expect should a side effect or adverse reaction occur.

It was not uncommon for sales reps to spend four weeks in training at the company headquarters, followed by two weeks of field training with a district sales manager and then an additional four weeks at the regional office. The duration and intensity of the training program were intended to prepare each rep for appropriate and effective interactions with office staff and physicians and, most importantly, to ensure that physicians would receive complete and accurate information about the company's products.

Graduation came with a sense of accomplishment and unwavering confidence. The rigorous training instilled pride in the company, reinforced the value of its products, and underscored the commitment made by the company to ensure the success of each rep. Training continued after graduation in an ongoing process consisting of quarterly district meetings and regular advanced training sessions or mini-internships at academic hospitals or clinics.

A sales rep's first days in the field were spent with the district sales manager. Managers provided instruction on all sorts of matters ranging from how to pack your trunk to how to organize your territory; they also reviewed the requirements for weekly reporting and conducted practice presentations. During an office visit, managers watched how the sales rep interacted with the office staff and physicians and provided candid and sometimes critical feedback (verbal and written) on every aspect of performance. This feedback or coaching allowed the new sales rep to take immediate corrective steps to ensure that physicians would have a positive experience, even with novices.

District sales managers were coaches, mentors, business managers, and sometimes even friends. They were held accountable for everything that happened in their districts, which comprised eight to twelve territories. Geography and physician concentration (and eventually physician prescribing volume) determined the sizes of territories and districts. The district sales manager was responsible for revenue generation (by exhorting the troops and leading by example), keeping track of all business expenses, regulatory and legal compliance, customer relations, and making sure products were available at pharmacies and hospitals serving his or her district.

Pharmaceutical sales positions rarely became available; most openings arose as a result of promotions, retirements, or the occasional termination. Partly due to this low turnover and to years of every other week or monthly office visits, a healthy professional relationship often developed between sales reps and the physicians they called on. Most offices did not require reps to make appointments, and the staff often felt bad if a rep had to wait to see the doctor. Access was driven by a rep's relationship with the physician and office staff, the information he or she provided, and the perceived value of the visit. Reps often provided drug samples (which were typically dispensed by physicians to indigent or elderly patients), patient education materials (e.g., brochures and anatomical models), and useful product reminders (e.g., pens, notepads, clipboards) as part of an ongoing effort to provide value, curry favor with the office staff, and increase the likelihood of seeing the doctor during the next visit.

Before the rapid expansion of sales forces, success (i.e., revenue generation and relationship building) was driven more by technical expertise and competence than anything else. It was essential for the rep to establish rapport and credibility as a trusted source of accurate product and disease-state information while demonstrating socially engaging and professional interpersonal skills. Reps who had good interpersonal skills but no corresponding product or disease-state knowledge usually had to turn to more desperate tactics in order to gain access to physicians, as will be discussed later. Although interpersonal skills were important, having a thorough knowledge of one's products as well as other therapeutic options, providing balanced (discussing safety as well as efficacy) presentations, and not criticizing the competition all were essential for establishing credibility. The establishment and maintenance of credibility required a level of expertise and professionalism that was earned through rigorous training, insightful field coaching by experienced district sales managers, and, most importantly, time in the field. Since it was possible for sales reps to ingratiate themselves to secure an audience with some physicians and their office staffs, time in the field and the ability to conduct intelligent and meaningful product discussions and build strong relationships based on mutual respect became the real tests of expertise and competence for a sales rep.

While selling skills were useful, many physicians found sales reps who relied solely on them to be disingenuous and manipulative. Nevertheless, the industry explored numerous techniques to help reps become more effective in their presentations. Persuasive techniques, including Socratic Selling® (customer-focused logical questioning which leads to a favorable sales outcome), pharmaceutical industry-tailored selling systems (usually created by outside companies), and even the more controversial application of neurolinguistic programming* became popular. Some of the more manipulative programs, many of which probably had no place in selling situations with physicians, were implemented with varying degrees of success.

Robust research pipelines produced a plethora of blockbuster products in the 1980s and through the 1990s, which led to an explosive growth in sales organizations (Figure 9-1), from hundreds of representatives per company to thousands; ultimately, five to ten thousand representatives became the norm for top revenue-producing companies such as Pfizer, Sanofi-Aventis, and GlaxoSmithKline. Maintaining the preference for hiring sales representatives with life-science degrees became more challenging, however, and the rigorous selection and training standards of the previous era became stressed to an unsustainable level. This growth forced companies to turn to uncharacteristically aggressive strategies for recruiting, training, and retaining their sales force. Some companies even supplemented their internal sales organizations by contracting with outside sales organizations. Sales force quality was further compromised by a lack of sufficiently trained and experienced sales managers who were needed to deploy these very large sales organizations. Typically, for every thousand sales representatives, one hundred district sales manag-

* Neurolinguistic programming (NLP) was developed in the 1970s by Richard Bandler and John Grinder as a form of psychological therapy that was based, in part, on overcoming learned limitations in order to influence one's own behavior patterns as well as those in others. NLP posited that only three behavior patterns provided the foundation for effective communication. NLP concepts continue to be discussed and presented in seminars, workshops, and self-help books and tapes.

Figure 9-1. The combined sales force size of the top forty pharmaceutical companies. Data from SDI, Yardley, Pennsylvania.

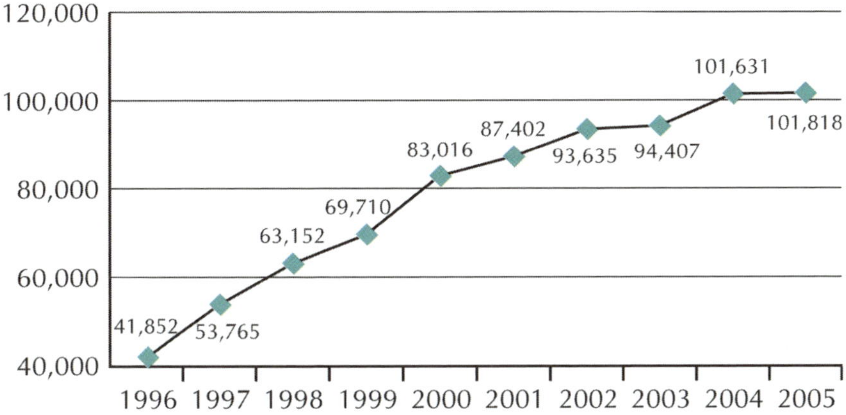

ers, ten regional sales managers, and one sales director were needed. The result was that some of the industry's best salespeople were promoted to managers (ironically, good salespeople don't necessarily make good managers) and, even worse, many less experienced sales representatives were prematurely promoted to managers, often with disastrous consequences.

Companies were faced with the prospect of rapid expansion in an industry that required ever-higher levels of industry-specific medical and scientific training, expertise, and competence. A sales arms race ensued, along with a concurrent diminution of expertise and competence, the effects of which are still being felt today. Even companies with the best training programs and the most experienced representatives could not keep up with their own growth, much less the demands of the industry as a whole; many of their best people became targets (by recruiters) for competitors. A cascade of unintended consequences followed. In order to grow their businesses, companies were forced to promote sales people prematurely, putting less experienced district sales managers in the position of having to hire less qualified applicants to fill sales positions. Often, these less qualified candidates had to be trained by less experienced trainers, because the experienced trainers were also being promoted prematurely to district sales managers or marketing positions. These less well-trained sales reps then went into the field to be coached by less experienced district sales managers who were often struggling in their own jobs. At the same time, because of the pressing need to get people into the field, training began to focus on essential product information, leaving less time, if any, to learn about disease states and therapeutic options, or to assimilate professional and ethical expectations for pharmaceutical sales reps. These deficiencies in training would later prove costly to the industry.

In an attempt to counter the diminishing level of training and expertise among sales reps in general, many companies developed specialty sales forces that received highly focused training to support their products in technically demanding therapeutic areas (e.g., cardiology, neuroscience, oncology). This strategy worked well until the demand for these representatives greatly exceeded the industry's ability to hire and train qualified new people to the level of expertise demanded by physicians in these highly demanding specialty markets.

Not surprisingly, physicians and office staffs noticed the massive increase in sales force numbers and attendant decrease in competence and professionalism. Some offices were bombarded with three or four sales reps from the same company hawking the same or different drugs. The response was a significant and selective reduction in access to physicians. An increasing number of physicians became known as "no-see" doctors, who refused to see any drug company representatives.

Restricted access led to a new wave of sales tactics. It was only a matter of time before a quid pro quo culture took hold in which all kinds of incentives and perks (many of which were nothing more than veiled bribes or kickbacks) were offered in exchange for access to physicians or provided as rewards for prescribing the company's products. It would not be overstating the case to say that sales reps would do almost anything to meet with high-volume prescribing physicians in their territories. The occasional casual business lunch was transformed into the obligatory "lunch and learn," which evolved into the now infamous "dine and dash" (drop off lunch without even seeing the physician). To secure an audience with physicians, reps began providing lunch not only for the physicians but for their office staffs as well. In many offices, this became the extorted toll for access. With sales reps from so many companies providing these lunches, office staffs began scheduling them as replacements for office calls and one-on-one discussions with physicians. Although many well-intentioned reps did their best to convert these sales opportunities into meaningful product presentations, the group lunch environment was simply not conducive to serious discussions about diseases and treatment options.

Diminished physician access also began to taint what started out as helpful giveaways or tchotchkes (a Yiddish term for relatively inexpensive items such as pens, sticky pads, clipboards, patient diaries, and anatomical models for patient counseling) for physicians, office staffs, and patients. Representatives supported by well-funded marketing departments resorted to increasingly expensive tchotchkes and gifts in return for physician access. Tickets to sporting or local cultural events, dinners at fancy restaurants, and financial support for local charities helped them gain access. Sales reps also began recommending physicians for clinical studies and inviting them to speak (for an honorarium) at company-sponsored local medical education dinner programs. In a relatively short period, the pharmaceutical sales rep was transformed from a valuable, credible source of product and disease information to a purveyor of meals, industry gifts, perks, and programs in exchange for access and as rewards for prescribing the company's drugs. While some physicians clearly found these activities disturbing, others and their office staffs learned how to create a competitive environment, pitting the tchotchkes and other perks from one company against those of another to further enhance the value of subsequent offerings.

This trend of socializing with physicians to gain business led some companies to hire new sales representatives based more on their professional appearance and social skills than on their technical competence. Disparagingly referred to as "Barbie and Ken" reps (even to this day), the trend drew considerable attention from the media and medical profession, and articles about "cheerleader reps" began to appear in newspapers and magazines. This characterization was not just figurative; it turned out that some pharmaceutical sales reps had indeed been college cheerleaders, while others were professional cheerleaders on weekends and pharmaceutical sales reps during the week.[1] The qualifications of these individuals notwithstanding, many sales managers had determined that employing personable, attractive young women as sales reps could increase the amount of face time and favorably influence prescribing by a predominantly male physician audience. Once again, the ends justified the means.

Physicians, many of whom could quickly discern a sales representative's level of product and disease-state knowledge, became ambivalent about canned industry messaging delivered by industry droids. The value of the sales representative's visits deteriorated as the seemingly endless number of less well-trained reps became walking company advertisements. Time with physicians diminished, as did access, with many sales calls resulting in an impersonal sample drop (leaving product samples with little or no interaction with the physician).

While the technical skills of sales reps were waning, the science behind the robust product pipelines that was driving the expansion in sales forces was becoming more challenging. Regardless of the intensity of training, without a strong science background, the sales rep was forced to rely to a greater and greater extent on company-scripted product presentations. Previously well-trained, relationship-oriented reps became frustrated by the lack of effective training and the increasingly limited access to physicians. By appointment only, scheduled rep visit times, and sitting in waiting rooms became common, even for the best sales reps.

The increasing visibility of quid pro quo sales tactics led to an increase in local restrictions in office practices and hospitals, especially those affiliated with managed care organizations and medical schools. In response, the industry, through the Pharmaceutical Research and Manufacturers of America (PhRMA*), tried to police itself by issuing self-imposed guidelines,[2] but it was a case of too little too late. Voluntary compliance and a lack of enforcement only encouraged some companies to ignore the guidelines in order to create a competitive advantage over those companies that were complying. In addition to the payer communities, state governments became involved in establishing their own restrictions on pharmaceutical promotions. Today, office giveaways have been banned, and restrictions have been placed on what reps can discuss with physicians (e.g., if your product is not on formulary, you can't discuss it with plan providers). Pharmaceutical sales reps have been banned from some institutions, while some states and the District of Columbia have mandated or are considering licensure or certification for sales reps.[3]

In this increasingly restrictive and hostile environment, pharmaceutical marketers became more desperate at trying to influence prescribing patterns. We have already discussed the results of several government investigations which revealed that to expand

* The primary industry trade group that represents most Big Pharma and many biotechnology companies.

the market for some products, sales reps had been trained and encouraged to sell products for indications that were not FDA-approved. This off-label promotion is illegal because it subverts the intent of FDA regulatory requirements for proving safety and efficacy. With the aid of whistleblowers in some cases, several companies have had to pay millions and even billions of dollars in settlements for these indiscretions. While sales reps had always walked a fine line in their discussions with physicians (and often crossed it during informal meetings or conversations), the decision to proactively encourage off-label promotional tactics revealed how desperate the industry was in its pursuit of revenue growth.

In recent years as product pipelines withered and generic drugs replaced brand-name drugs, access to physicians was curtailed further, and regulatory constraints on what can be discussed diminished the value of the traditional sales rep and resulted in a corresponding trend toward sales force downsizing. The shift in prescribing influence from physicians to institutional payers has also taken its toll. The result has been monthly, if not weekly, announcements of layoffs among pharmaceutical sales reps in an ongoing attempt to reduce costs by matching the size of the sales force with the realities of the market. It seems that the heyday of the traditional pharmaceutical sales rep has passed.

The evolving new healthcare market represents an opportunity for pharmaceutical companies to regroup and rethink their sales models. For the foreseeable future, it will remain the industry's responsibility to develop acceptable (to the market) and effective ways of informing physicians and healthcare providers about the risks versus the benefits of new drug treatments. Despite claims to the contrary, most healthcare institutions and organization, including medical schools and health maintenance organizations, have little or no incentive, capacity for, or interest in developing programs to educate community-based healthcare practitioners about the details of new prescription drugs. As medicine continues to build on advances in the basic sciences and technology, more technically advanced drugs will become available to treat more diseases at the molecular level. The era of personalized medicine, when drugs will be tailor-made to an individual's genetic blueprint, is not far off.* The science behind these new products and the data that form the basis for their FDA approval

* The recently approved vaccine for advanced prostate cancer (Provenge®, sipuleucel-T) is a prototypical example of a personalized treatment.

and use will require a much higher level of medical information than traditional promotional messaging can (or should) deliver. All of this suggests that the innovative new products of the future will not be amenable to the simplistic "one message fits all" mass marketing campaigns of the past.

Against a backdrop of growing intolerance for pharmaceutical sales people, a diminishing role of physicians in product selection, fewer mass-market products, and an increasingly managed market, large traditional sales organizations are a thing of the past. In the evolving new healthcare market, pharmaceutical sales should be replaced by two new independent roles. The first will be a national accounts and managed care role to ensure that new products are included on plan formularies, made available to patients with few restrictions, and reimbursed by insurers with reasonable co-pays. Individuals fulfilling this role will be responsible for account customer service, formulating account strategies, and leading all negotiations regarding price. Their primary job will be to ensure the company is meeting the needs of its customers. The other role will consist of individuals who provide technical, scientific, and medical expertise to ensure that healthcare provider plans, physicians, and patients understand the appropriate use, potential risks, and relative value (versus other therapeutic options) of products. These new positions will be filled by individuals with advanced life-science degrees (MDs, RNs, or PharmDs) who also have narrow but in-depth therapeutic expertise and advanced medical training. Reporting to Medical Affairs in Research, these individuals will ensure the appropriate use of drugs in the context of overall patient care and other therapeutic options available. Neither one of these new roles will be referred to as sales positions nor will they be compensated based on sales revenues.

For better or for worse, pharmaceutical sales representatives have always been in the vanguard of commercialization efforts. However, many of the tactics they employed over the years are no longer acceptable or effective in today's healthcare environment. The rapid pace of advances in science and medicine will lead to more technically challenging products that will require companies to find better ways to effectively disseminate information about these products. Individuals with the educational background, therapeutic expertise, and ability to convey this information to healthcare providers will be highly sought after. Companies that understand these changes and work to redefine the role of the sales rep will have a distinct advantage over their competitors.

Chapter 10
The Pharmaceutical Marketing Game

The importance of marketing to a pharmaceutical company's bottom line cannot be overestimated. Marketing campaigns have turned mediocre products into commercial successes and created blockbuster drugs with sustainable revenue streams even when few differences existed between these drugs and their competition. Nevertheless, the role that pharmaceutical marketing plays is often misunderstood and even reviled by those outside the industry and, surprisingly, marketing gets little respect even within the industry itself.

While marketing has always played a major role in bolstering the financial success of the pharmaceutical industry, during the past twenty years or so, the questionable and sometimes illegal tactics employed by pharmaceutical marketers have greatly contributed to the public's negative perception of the industry. Like their effect on expertise in pharmaceutical sales discussed in the previous chapter, booming pipelines and rapid organizational growth also resulted in a diminution in available marketing competence. The industry, desperate to support new product launches, could not provide its hordes of inexperienced marketing personnel with sufficient training to keep up with the demand for marketing expertise. This deficiency in expertise and competence, combined with a lack of diligent, experienced management oversight, led to strategic and promotional missteps, wasteful spending, and, ultimately, serious legal and regulatory problems.

Prior to the explosive growth of the 1980s and 1990s, pharmaceutical marketers often came up through the ranks of the existing sales organization; they were trained in-house and were mentored by seasoned veterans over the course of several years. While some may have had marketing degrees, it was still expected that they would spend time in the field before being promoted to a marketing position. While not all good salespeople would necessarily become good marketers, the sales force was a logical source for marketing candidates and provided a natural, experience-based career path for those interested in a future position in corporate management. Sales reps with several years of experience and a successful track record of revenue generation and relationship building brought fresh, real-world thinking and a pragmatic approach to marketing planning. Industry insiders could always identify someone who had "carried the bag" (sales reps carried detail bags containing product literature and samples), because their field experience provided them with a clear view of the problems that physicians faced in trying to provide therapeutic relief to their patients. Sales reps often possessed an almost intuitive grasp of how best to influence physician decision-making processes and were aware of and sensitive to the growing influence of insurance companies and government programs on physician prescribing practices. And perhaps more than anyone else at the company, sales reps also understood that if they performed well in their jobs, more patients would benefit by receiving the right drugs at the right doses. This understanding of the physician-patient dynamic played a key role in helping former reps develop effective marketing strategies and programs.

As sales organizations continued to grow, the pool of competent marketing candidates with sufficient sales training and field experience contracted. Despite their best efforts to screen candidates, many companies—in an effort to keep up with demand—began to indiscriminately offer marketing positions to good salespeople, many of whom, in retrospect, should have stayed in sales. Some accepted the promotions out of fear of being passed over for future advancement (i.e., "if I don't accept this, I may not be offered another promotion"), while others were just looking to climb the corporate ladder. Some salespeople, who were used to having autonomy in their own territories, had misperceptions about the marketing job function and found it difficult to be effective and productive in a corporate bureaucracy.

Many companies tried to enhance and supplement their corporate marketing expertise by sending some of their sales and marketing managers to executive MBA programs or by recruiting newly minted MBAs from some of the most prestigious business schools in the country. Given the fact that attending executive MBA classes was essentially a second full-time job, one has to wonder how effectively these managers performed in their day jobs. Although the newly minted MBAs had received better training in marketing than those who came directly from sales, many lacked meaningful field experience, and few had any appreciable understanding of the pharmaceutical industry. Some companies tried to offset these deficiencies by requiring these individuals to obtain short-term (typically one to two years) sales experience before moving them into marketing positions. The increasing demand for pharmaceutical marketers, however, was still far greater than the supply and resulted in ever shorter stints in the field—often less than one year. This gradual reduction in the field experience of marketing managers, which occurred over several decades, led to an industry-wide diminution in marketing expertise and competence at a time when both the complexities of the healthcare market as well as the need for scientific and technical expertise were increasing.

As a result of having spent insufficient time in the position and not having benefited from experienced mentoring, many new marketers were unable to develop an adequate level of expertise which led to serious mistakes and poor decisions, the most apparent (at least to the outside world) of which resulted in major legal and regulatory problems. These industry-wide problems culminated in diminished market credibility and a loss of public trust and confidence in the industry. Because marketing directs all commercial activities and influences many other corporate functions including R&D, the consequences of diminished expertise and competence in this area were far-reaching; indeed, it would not be an exaggeration to say that the indiscretions and mistakes perpetrated by marketing managers over the past two decades have had the most damaging effects on the industry's image and credibility.

Before we describe exactly what happened, it is important to understand the fundamental responsibilities of pharmaceutical marketing. The job entails a multitude of day-to-day tasks from strategic planning and production forecasting to the development of advertising and promotion programs. Marketing managers (also referred to as product managers) are typically responsible for the following:

1. Marketing planning based on a thorough understanding of their product and therapeutic area, competitive products (both current and future), the legal and regulatory environments, and anticipated near- and long-term challenges;

2. Development of strategies and tactics that effectively and efficiently maximize the commercial potential of marketed products while delivering a reasonable return on investment (ROI);
3. Ensuring compliance with all state and federal regulations and laws;
4. Developing and funding activities that enhance the product brand and the company's image;
5. Assisting R&D with portfolio management by helping to prioritize projects, establishing the product profile (e.g., characteristics, features, and benefits) that will meet or exceed future market needs, and ensuring that clinical development trial designs provide the data to support the commercial claims and anticipated competitive advantages of the new product.

At its most basic level, "knowing your product and your market" as well as insightful strategic planning are at the heart of good marketing campaigns. Such campaigns typically begin with a market analysis, including a description of the market, the disease, and treatment options (both current and anticipated), and a so-called product SWOT (strengths, weaknesses, opportunities, and threats) analysis. This analysis is essential to providing credible commercial input to R&D, making sound strategic decisions, and determining what to emphasize in advertising and promotional programs.

One of the biggest challenges to the industry is the interpretation of increasing volumes of data. The industry has a vast amount of information at its disposal, including the prescribing habits of physicians and the purchasing practices of its customers, which it uses to identify and assess market opportunities, formulate commercialization strategies, and develop forecast models. Market research has become increasingly sophisticated with techniques that delve into the psychology of prescribing, the effectiveness of electronic media and the power of graphic design, and the science underlying persuasive techniques.

The ability to gather information retrospectively and to quantitatively project the future has become a powerful modeling tool that provided a sense of intellectual comfort for marketers with MBAs. As a result, in recent years market analysis and spreadsheet modeling began to dominate the marketing planning process. These spreadsheet-based analytics and their conclusions were presented (or, worse yet, accepted) as facts, with little consideration of the impact of missing historical data, flawed assumptions, the nuances of prescribing decisions, or the long-term implications of decisions that relied on these analyses. These omissions were particularly serious when it came to new products in new therapeutic categories; in these cases most variables were filled in with data from similar historical situations, results from comparable products, or best guesses.

Even with established products in well-defined markets, many non-quantitative factors had to be plugged in to these models. For example, quantifying the nuances of treatment—such as the influence of laboratory data on prescribing habits, the likelihood of formulary acceptance of a new product over time, and the level of patient satisfaction with a new product—is challenging at best, and much less quantifiable without best-guess assumptions. These best guesses are based on interpretations of qualitative data, industry experience, and market insight. However, best guesses by marketers with limited experience and a lack of market insight became increasingly less accurate and their forecasts less reliable, which led to flawed models, exaggerated revenue forecasts, and unrealistic market (think Wall Street investors) expectations. These flawed forecasts made it more difficult for marketers and salespeople to deliver the expected results, and some resorted to increasingly aggressive (and often illegal) tactics in an effort to meet these unrealistic expectations.

Despite glaring limitations, these analytics often provided senior executives with a quantitative security blanket for making decisions, especially when they lacked the necessary market insight or expertise to perform their own analyses. These data were also frequently used as the basis for tactical plans (i.e., how many sales calls were needed, which journals to advertise in, and how many samples were required to convert an account). With flawed input or data interpretation, good decisions were compromised in the tactical planning process as well, leading to inappropriate and wasteful spending on programs and projects.

The industry's more recent foray into direct-to-consumer (DTC)* advertising (on television and the Internet) is perhaps one

* DTC advertising utilizes direct mail, consumer magazines, the Internet including social media websites, and television ads often featuring prominent celebrities hawking specific prescription drugs.

of the best examples of this profligacy: collectively, the industry spent $4.5 billion on DTC advertising in 2009.[1] With the plethora of medical information now readily available to consumers, there is considerable debate over how effective these ads really are at persuading patients to request specific products or discuss a specific medical condition with their physicians. One study that evaluated the impact of DTC advertising found that 12,500 patient-doctor conversations in 2008 resulted in only 23 specific drug requests by patients.[2] Another study, however, demonstrated a median increase in sales of $2.20 for every DTC dollar of advertising, while a third study indicated that only 2% to 7% of consumers who saw a DTC ad requested and ultimately received a prescription for the advertised drug.[3] Perhaps the most disturbing study of DTC advertising, reported in the *Archives of Internal Medicine*, indicated that while DTC advertising for Plavix® (clopidogrel) had no apparent effect on prescribing, it did result in a sudden and sustained increase in the cost per unit drug of $0.40 after the start of DTC advertising, which resulted in an additional $207 million in pharmacy expenditures.[4] And yet, DTC ads continue to appear on television (one for a smoking cessation product is a full 2 ½ minutes in length), despite continuing questions about their appropriateness, cost, and effectiveness.

The increased focus on market analysis and tactical planning meant less time was devoted to the much harder work of strategy development that required expertise and market insight. With fewer clinically differentiated products being introduced, knowledge of the market and relevant therapeutic areas became even more critical in terms of formulating and assessing creative strategic options and developing insightful and unique product positioning messages (how a product is perceived by the market relative to other products). As a result, the development of creative and impactful brand messages became the exception rather than the rule for those marketers with limited expertise and competence. Moreover, because of their inexperience (and the belief that they knew more than they actually did), many could not recognize creative and effective messages even when they were presented to them by outside sources, often putting them at odds with the advertising agency they hired in the first place. This conflict is best illustrated by wordy journal ads or ads in which the graphics do not agree with the words—clear signs of a novice marketer. Nevertheless, pharmaceutical marketers pay advertising agencies to develop their creative messages, and the marketers ultimately have the final say.

With superficial interpretations of the market and questionable projections and market forecasts, it did not take long before R&D personnel lost confidence in the recommendations they were receiving from their marketing counterparts. This situation was particularly frustrating for research scientists whose discussions with practicing clinicians often contradicted the information they received from their marketing colleagues. These contradictions, coupled with the short tenure of product managers (often less than a couple of years), contributed to a sense that marketing people were intellectual lightweights who were in way over their heads, and in many instances this was indeed the case. The failures of these corporate marketers might not have had such negative consequences in another industry, but in an industry that dealt with the health and, in many instances, the very lives of its customers, one would expect marketers to be more concerned with the needs of healthcare providers and their patients than anything else.

The commercialization objective of pharmaceutical marketing is to create a positive market image or brand that allows physicians, patients, and the market to immediately and positively associate a product name or logo with its therapeutic application and benefits in the context of its competitors (i.e., establishing its position). For example, Lipitor® (atorvastatin), marketed by Pfizer, is immediately recognizable as a drug used to treat high cholesterol, in part because its name is derived from the word lipid, which refers to fats and oils. Lipitor® product branding is one of the most successful examples of good pharmaceutical marketing and represents a major accomplishment, especially in the commercially noisy world of healthcare. Strong product positioning and a brand that is supported by a well-crafted strategy and communications plan are also the basis for market-sensitive pricing (understanding the price points at which the market converts from acceptance to tolerance to resentment) and allow for a more efficient (spending smaller amounts of money on strategically effective programs to yield higher sales results) advertising and promotional campaign to be developed.

One of the most important aspects of branding is tactical execution (i.e., deploying advertising and promotional activities that raise market awareness, establish the product's position, stimulate sales, and support the brand; see highlight box on page 95). Traditional pharmaceutical tactics include journal advertising, direct mail, sponsorship of seminars, hosting exhibits at professional conferences,* and, more recently, television commercials and web-based advertising. The sales organization has historically represented one of the largest tactical expenses ($12 billion for the industry in 2008), accounting for more than half of the industry's marketing budgets.[5] Pharmaceutical sales teams were traditionally given large discretionary budgets (often thousands of dollars per month) for lunch-and-learn meetings, speaker programs, local medical conferences, and support of local charities. Individual reps were armed with a surfeit of marketing brochures, office trinkets, and product samples, all paid for with marketing dollars. The goals of these marketing tactics were to help raise awareness about a product or a disease, create interest in the product, and provide accurate and balanced information to physicians while producing a positive brand image. If physicians associated the product's brand name with its FDA-approved indication, then these activities were producing the desired effect, and if the product's name was the first to come to mind when patients presented with the approved indication, the marketing and sales team had really done its job well.

Before we delve into the collective impact of diminished marketing expertise on the industry, it should be acknowledged that the industry has launched many blockbuster products over

* According to the Congressional Budget Office,[5] U.S. pharmaceutical companies spent $3.4 billion sponsoring professional meetings and events to advertise and promote their products in 2008. This expenditure included exhibits and presentations of results (at least the favorable ones) of studies carried out with their drugs. Organizations such as the American College of Cardiology (ACC), the American College of Gastroenterology (ACG), the American College of Rheumatology (ACR), the American Society of Clinical Oncology (ASCO), the Interscience Conference on Antimicrobial Agents and Chemotherapy (ICAAC), the Radiological Society of North America (RSNA), and many others hold large annual meetings for their members, the industries that support them, and the press. The exhibition booths at these events are manned by company employees who provide company literature and other materials to meeting attendees. Industry-sponsored continuing medical education programs, receptions, and dinners were held for physician-attendees as part of an ongoing effort to demonstrate support for professional societies, and these programs also help influence large numbers of prescribers at a single event. In the past year or so, however, many of these activities have been curtailed or banned altogether.

the years and has been able to extract double-digit price increases from the market. These successes can be attributed to at least one of the following: a great product with the science to support the differences between it and other therapeutic options, effective marketing and sales programs, or promotional budgets large enough to overwhelm the competition. Along the way, however, aggressive marketers unleashed an endless stream of new ways to convince physicians to prescribe mediocre, undifferentiated me-too products (drugs with similar chemical structures to existing drugs and similar therapeutic applications). Not surprisingly, many of these revenue-generating tactics infuriated the market, alienated physicians, and produced legal and regulatory liabilities, all of which led to greatly reduced credibility and trust.

Many companies provide advertising, promotional, and educational services to the pharmaceutical industry—from high-profile New York advertising agencies (which can generate tens of millions of dollars in billing), to publishers and little-known communications companies (many located close to pharmaceutical company headquarters in New York, New Jersey, and eastern Pennsylvania) that provide various educational services, to "boutique" companies that sell the throwaway items that sales reps hand out, to free-lance writers who provide ghostwriting and other writing services. In a long-overdue move, some medical journals are now requiring authors to provide information about the provenance of any manuscript submitted and are refusing to publish articles that are ghostwritten. Virtually all individuals and companies that provide these services are referred to as "vendors" and are part of the food chain that serves the pharmaceutical industry. Physicians (particularly key opinion leaders, or KOLs; see footnote on p. 99) who speak on behalf of and provide consulting services to the industry are at the top of the food chain, while free-lancers are at the bottom. Drug companies and their sales reps will go to almost any length to satisfy these KOLs. In general, vendors (other than physician vendors) receive little respect from the pharmaceutical industry, in part because they do not have the power to negatively impact sales. This is one reason why vendors, who are often asked to submit proposals by prospective clients, never receive the courtesy of a reply. Pharmaceutical companies may also ask vendors and free-lancers to work with physician-consultants on various projects; in these situations the vendor (or free-lancer) has two masters: the pharmaceutical company that pays the bill and the physician-consultant. Failure to satisfy either one will usually result in loss of work for the vendor. Other than providing advice or refusing to do the work, vendors can do little to keep pharmaceutical companies from engaging in unethical business practices or other wrongdoing. The code of business ethics that many pharmaceutical companies display in their lobbies notwithstanding, their message to vendors is quite clear: either play ball, do as we say, or forget about working for us. So why do vendors work with these companies? Because they spend large sums of money promoting their products and the potential rewards often far outweigh the aggravation.

As has been repeatedly demonstrated, effective marketing can create a preference for branded products even when generic or over-the-counter alternatives are available at lower prices. However, a lack of marketing expertise can lead to misinterpretation of market analytics, simplistic strategies that lack creativity, and inappropriate or ineffective communications plans and tactics. Moreover, deploying the wrong tactics to an unreceptive audience leads to a need for more tactics, more resources, and larger budgets in an effort to generate the same level of revenue. Marketing incompetence can also create confusion and negative brand perceptions, a situation that is particularly challenging for sales representatives as they desperately try to convince an increasingly recalcitrant and skeptical market that they have a safe and effective product. While well-funded but poorly crafted marketing programs may have helped deliver remarkable sales results in the past, these tactics will not work in a much less forgiving and more managed healthcare environment. Not only will companies find it more difficult to justify higher spending to offset mediocre marketing programs for expensive drugs, but, more importantly, they will reinforce customer perceptions of wasteful spending, create negative brand images, and instill resentment toward those products and their perceived unjustified high prices. Perhaps partly out of fear the market would soon wise up, in the midst of public concerns about rising healthcare costs in a slow-growing economy with unemployment hovering at around 10%, the industry increased branded drug prices by 9.3% in 2009.[6]

So what really happens at the functional level when marketing tasks are carried out by product managers with budgets often in the tens of millions of dollars but who lack the necessary expertise to do their job and who are more interested in driving sales than in anything else? Here are some of the implications of this situation:

1. Inexperienced marketers rely almost entirely on their advertising agency of record. This approach permeates everything from market analysis and strategy development to drafting marketing plans and developing budgets that are driven by the advertising and promotion plans proposed by the agency. In a very real sense, this is an excellent example of the fox guarding the chicken coop. Pharmaceutical companies pay dearly for this reckless outsourcing, paying huge markups on just about everything the agency does while the agency generates addi-

tional revenue from the changes ordered by indecisive and/or inexperienced product managers.

2. Products do not receive the benefit of comprehensive strategic planning. Knowledge of the marketing planning process is undermined by the lack of critical thinking in interpreting market data and developing strategic options. What tends to get done well are the relatively easy tasks of gathering market data and modeling tactical plans and budgets based on what was done the previous year or on other products. For some marketers, there is no discernable difference between strategy and tactics.
3. Promotional messages and advertising campaigns are less strategic, lack impact, and ultimately waste money as marketers increase advertising budgets to compensate for poor copy, meaningless graphics, and inefficient use of advertising agency resources.
4. Drug pricing becomes less strategic, less value-based, and driven more by what the market will bear. With little value-enhancing data (e.g., cost savings from fewer hospitalizations or improved quality of life) to support pricing, the price of the drug is perceived as unjustifiably high.
5. The lack of expertise translates into little or no meaningful guidance or feedback for vendors and suppliers. Inexperienced product managers tend to have little or no respect for vendors and suppliers and don't know how to tap into vendor expertise. This mentality might change if all would-be marketers were required to do an internship on the vendor side for at least three months.
6. Commercial input to R&D becomes simplistic, nonstrategic, or even misleading. Unfortunately, the least experienced marketers are often sent to R&D as a training exercise, which leads to comments from researchers such as, "Thank you for telling us you would like orange tablets and not yellow capsules." Those in research and development who have lived and breathed the product from its inception quickly recognize the limited knowledge of inexperienced product managers and their corresponding lack of marketing expertise. As scientists, they are also unimpressed by the qualitative assumptions used to support quantitative spreadsheet model-driven conclusions. They politely ignore commercial input that lacks

credibility. Unfortunately, this lack of meaningful marketing input leads to clinical trial designs and product profiles that may satisfy regulatory requirements but do not address important commercial considerations. One of the biggest marketing challenges occurs when clinical data fail to support research claims of superiority compared to other drugs in the same therapeutic class (often the rationale for developing the new product in the first place). A lack of insightful marketing input can ultimately lead to products that are more difficult to commercialize as well as serious product launch failures.

7. Regulatory issues regarding advertising and promotion become liabilities as ambitious marketers with little expertise unknowingly venture into regulatory minefields, relying on their advertising agencies or in-house medical-legal review teams to keep them compliant.
8. A lack of organizational credibility places the inexperienced marketing person in a difficult position when taking the other side of internally popular positions, such as objecting to management's suggestion to be more aggressive with promotion and push the regulatory envelope (i.e., see how far you can go without getting caught). Marketers who lack expertise and organizational credibility may also find it difficult to convince senior management that a new product may not be as commercially viable as R&D has led them to believe, even in those instances in which the inexperienced marketer is correct.
9. Effective marketing in the United States is challenging even for the best of marketers, but launching a product globally becomes almost impossible for the inexperienced marketer. Differences in market dynamics (i.e., how healthcare is provided), prescribing habits, the role that competitive products play in the market, cultural nuances (e.g., color and symbol implications), accepted sales and marketing tactics, and regulatory requirements all add complexity that requires global marketing expertise.
10. Unfortunately, marketing managers with limited expertise become role models and mentors for new hires, leading to a progressive deterioration in expertise, expectations, and competence, regardless of the marketing expertise and experience of the rookie.

The implications of corporate vulnerabilities in these areas became apparent as organizational pressure for financial results combined with the inexperience of marketing personnel led to questionable and in some cases blatantly illegal marketing activities. A good example can be found in the way Medical Science Liaisons (MSLs) were sometimes utilized. Historically, the primary mission of these highly trained specialists was to help key opinion leaders (KOLs)* stay current with the latest information regarding diseases, treatment options, and research in their therapeutic areas of expertise. Before the Internet, MSLs performed a valuable service at a time when pharmaceutical companies had ready access to more information than was usually available from even the best medical school libraries. Once marketers realized the influence that MSLs could have in the marketplace, they deployed them as glorified sales representatives for pre-approval promotion of products in development and to promote marketed products for off-label uses. One of the most blatant cases discussed earlier occurred when Warner-Lambert deployed MSLs as part of a comprehensive marketing program to promote Neurontin® (an anti-epilepsy drug) for a variety of off-label uses. Pfizer, which acquired Warner-Lambert in 2000, agreed to a settlement of $430 million for this marketing fiasco.[7] Not only were these activities found to be illegal, but they also provided a public platform on which the motives, credibility, and scientific integrity of all industry commercialization tactics (good and bad) could be called into question.

Another marketing misstep was the transformation of once scientifically credible continuing medical education (CME) programs into shameless promotional events (see highlight box on next page). Despite the diminished scientific integrity associated with these programs, their promotional impact proved addicting to pharmaceutical marketers, who increased the number of such programs to the point where sales representatives spent as much

* KOLs are physicians who are considered experts in their respective fields. Reaching out to KOLs is based on the belief (by marketers) that if enough KOLs in a therapeutic area make positive statements about a particular drug, other physicians with less experience with that drug will generally follow suit (the trickle-down theory of marketing). Companies make use of KOLs in part to convince community-based physicians to change their prescribing patterns. Needless to say, the cumulative dollar amount that companies pay for these KOLs is significant.

time on meeting planning for these programs as they did on lunch-and-learn programs and certainly more time than they spent making product presentations to physicians. Marketers and salespeople found no shortage of physicians who were willing to supplement their regular income with speaker honoraria.

Over time, however, due to the frequency and plethora of program choices (virtually every company had programs for most of their products), sales reps found it increasingly difficult to secure audiences for their programs. In order to entice physicians to attend, more programs were held at upscale restaurants or in conjunction with popular sporting events. Some companies opted for resort locations and offered free trips to the Caribbean or subsidized physician expenses to attend professional meetings in order to secure an audience. Strategic marketing gave way to flagrant inducement tactics and share-of-voice (the company with the most visible marketing won) battles with ever increasing budgets to support more programs in even more enticing settings.

Eventually these programs lost credibility as it became apparent to the attendees that some of the physician-speakers were not necessarily experts in their fields. It also became clear that many physicians were willing to sell their professional and scientific integrity in return for lucrative speakers' fees (thousands of dollars per program) and all-expense-paid trips to exotic resorts for speaker training. In a page right out of the professional sports playbook, many physician-consultants pitted one pharmaceutical

---

Continuing medical education programs are typically offered by medical schools that are accredited by the Accreditation Council for Continuing Medical Education (ACCME), which sets standards for these programs in the United States. The ACCME is comprised of seven member organizations including the American Board of Medical Specialties, the American Hospital Association, the American Medical Association, the Association of American Medical Colleges, the Association for Hospital Medical Education, the Council of Medical Specialty Societies, and the Federation of State Medical Boards. Until recently, for-profit companies could apply for ACCME accreditation; if approved, these companies could then develop *and* approve CME programs. Still other for-profit companies that were accredited by the ACCME specialized in "accrediting" CME programs developed by companies that either did not want to navigate through the maze of requirements (and out-of-pocket expense) required to obtain accreditation from an ACCME-accredited medical school or could not obtain accreditation from a medical school. In the current legal-regulatory environment, most pharmaceutical companies no longer provide grants for CME programs that are not sponsored by accredited medical schools.

company against another in negotiating the best deals for their services. In fact, many of these physician-consultants became known pejoratively as "drug whores"[8] who appeared willing to speak or consult for any pharmaceutical company if the price was right. Increasing public disclosure requirements and litigation revealed that some physicians were collecting tens of thousands of dollars annually in advisory, consulting, and speaking fees.[9] It wasn't until questions were raised by industry critics about the potential for conflicts of interest and how all of this might be contributing to increasing drug prices that these programs began to fall into disfavor.

As a result of these and other marketing abuses, there has been a gradual overhaul with progressively more restrictive constraints on commercial support of CME programs. In 2008, the AMA's Council on Ethical and Judicial Affairs recommended a ban on commercial support, and more recently, at a hearing of the Senate Committee on Aging, critics lambasted the current CME environment as one that commingles marketing and education. One prominent industry critic, Dr. Steven Nissen, chairman of cardiovascular medicine at the Cleveland Clinic, testified that the federal government could save $900 billion over a ten-year period by curbing commercial bias in CME programs, many of which attempt to influence physicians to prescribe more higher-priced branded products.[10]

Today, despite the rapid pace at which new developments in medicine are occurring and the need for physicians and other healthcare providers to stay current, it is now more difficult than ever to secure CME grants from pharmaceutical companies. According to the Accreditation Council for Continuing Medical Education, commercial support (mostly from pharmaceutical companies but also from medical device companies) for CME, which accounts for 55% of CME funding in the United States, fell 11% to $1.3 billion in 2008.[11] In fact, most companies now have firewalls between their marketing and CME grants departments. At most companies, grant requests must now be submitted online, presumably to avoid any conflicts of interest between the prospective grantee and the grantor. Nevertheless, even with these safeguards, the negative implications associated with pharmaceutical industry-sponsored CME programs may ultimately put an end to them, another casualty of the abusive tactics employed by pharmaceutical marketers in their unending quest for revenue growth, larger market share, and higher profits. Evidence for this dramatic change in CME support can be seen in announcements by GlaxoSmithKline and Pfizer that they will no longer support CME activities developed and organized by commercial providers.[12,13] Nevertheless, Pfizer's recent attempt to redefine how CME is funded by providing Stanford University with a $3 million unrestricted medical education grant in early 2010 has been met with considerable skepticism.[14]

From a revenue perspective, traditional commercial tactics, which included aggressive marketing campaigns, were quite successful in generating substantial growth. As marketing tactics became more and more aggressive, serious regulatory and legal non-compliance issues were looming on the horizon. Without meaningful regulatory intervention, inexperienced sales and marketing personnel as well as senior management continued to believe that these activities had become accepted business practices in the pharmaceutical industry. While some companies were clearly more aggressive and brazen than others, there appeared to be an industry-wide acceptance of these marginally compliant and often illegal programs. This corporate disregard for compliance reinforced industry arrogance and led some pharmaceutical marketers to consider a notice of non-compliance from the FDA as a badge of honor for having pushed the regulatory envelope, while others considered it part of the cost of doing business. Once again, in the industry, the ends justified the means.

The pharmaceutical industry took full advantage of the FDA's complacency in policing and managing these commercialization indiscretions. A prudent individual would have thought that the negative press and associated customer concerns would have provided sufficient motivation for the industry to consider reevaluating their questionable activities. Yet, even in the face of massive fraud, false claims, and kickback litigation, the industry continues to push the envelope, probably because the financial burden of even billion-dollar settlements is still insignificant in the context of blockbuster product billion-dollar annual sales streams and the enormous cash troves of Big Pharma. Perhaps if pharmaceutical companies were forced to return *all* of the profits derived from their illegal activities, and any executives who knew (or should have known) about these tactics were forced to return all bonuses and stock options awarded during the time these activities took place, the win-at-any-cost mentality that drives these behaviors would fall into disfavor. At the very least, this punitive action would probably succeed in getting the attention of those executives whose compensation would be at risk and might lead to more rigorous management oversight and intervention to ensure regulatory and legal compliance.

In this chapter, we have provided some examples of how rapid industry growth led to the placement of inexperienced personnel in critical corporate marketing positions that resulted in a series of unintended consequences including dubious marketing planning, bloated budgets, inefficient use of resources, and loss of credibility. Diminished pharmaceutical commercialization expertise also led to the unfortunate gutting of once respected educational programs, serious concerns about financial payments to physicians, overt regulatory non-compliance, and costly and inefficient marketing campaigns. Collectively, these missteps have infuriated many groups and led to regulation and market-imposed constraints on pharmaceutical advertising and promotion. Perhaps even more importantly, these missteps and outrageous tactics have compromised public trust and provided both federal and state authorities with a platform of documented abuse which can (and no doubt will) form the basis for future litigation. In the future, inexperienced marketers will find the evolving new healthcare market even more challenging and much less forgiving.

Chapter 11
Pharmaceutical Research: The Lifeblood of the Industry

An extensive pipeline of commercially viable new products is the foundation upon which long-term success in the pharmaceutical industry is based. In the early days of the industry (following the Drug Efficacy Amendment of 1962), companies typically prided themselves on their ability to attract and employ some of the best research scientists in the world. If they needed people who had a particular expertise, they acquired or collaborated with them, regardless of the cost. Academic researchers were enticed by the quality of the facilities, the scientific challenges, and the salaries the companies were willing to pay. Many also had a desire to contribute to the creation of drugs with real-world applications that could produce actual benefits for patients.

Drug discovery has long relied on applied research that systematically matched natural products and chemicals with biologic systems in order to find ways to alter disease processes. Many successful products—from penicillin to taxol—have resulted from pairing the right compounds with the right disease states. Although a few drug discoveries may have been serendipitous (e.g., penicillin, chlordiazepoxide, sildenafil), in most cases scientific and medical expertise was required to appreciate the significance of the findings and, more importantly, to realize the potential utility of the new discoveries for treating disease. The pharmaceutical companies came to understand that the more they knew about the pathophysiology of diseases and the compounds being evaluated, the higher the probability of finding the right fit. Therefore, the companies sought expertise in medicine and the basic sciences (biology, chemistry, biochemistry) to help them find new treatments and understand how they worked.

As the industry grew, the finite pool of medical and scientific expertise was spread more and more thinly as more companies explored more therapeutic areas. Multidisciplinary teams of scientists gave way to promising new drug discovery tools that made it easier to "invent" new molecules and test them against known disease targets. Researchers used powerful computers to test structure-activity relationships and to build new compounds that would interact with biological targets. Computer-assisted automated robotic systems (also called high-throughput screening systems) allowed researchers to screen and investigate libraries that contained millions of chemical structures against hundreds of molecular targets looking for "hits" or some indication of a useful interaction. At the same time, the sciences of molecular biology, genomics, and proteomics took drug discovery to new heights, while sequencing of the human genome allowed for the possibility of devising cures for genetic disorders.

Ironically, these scientific advances seemed to diminish the need for understanding the pathophysiology of diseases in order to find potential therapeutics. The industry gradually redirected the focus of its pharmaceutical research away from the comprehensive investigation of the biochemistry and pathophysiology of disease to the hit-or-miss approach to finding drug candidates using laboratory-driven screening assays that had the potential to reveal promising compounds. Significant investments in laboratory facilities and instrumentation with large staffs of scientists and technicians supported the new R&D paradigm. Once a promising compound was discovered, it was easy for chemists to modify its chemical structure and develop a range of slightly different compounds in an effort to improve upon the physical characteristics (e.g., solubility), efficacy, and safety of the parent drug. Trial and error animal testing of these compounds then provided preliminary safety and dosing information for subsequent clinical trials.

Over the past few decades, this screening model seems to have run its course, and modification of known structures has begun to fall short in terms of meeting market expectations for innovation. Therefore, companies are now looking for new ways to discover the innovative new therapeutic agents of the future. Many are utilizing multidisciplinary systems biology (harnessing various fields such as chemistry, computer science, engineering, molecular biology, and physics) and synthetic biology (which involves literally creating biological molecules from scratch) to better understand the science behind human diseases and discover new ways of intervening in the disease process. Clearly, these are all steps in the right direction.

The ability to develop useful new products is inextricably linked to the quality and expertise of pharmaceutical research and development teams. As understanding of the molecular basis of diseases has increased, so too has the demand for drug researchers who can comprehend and interpret this information and its implications for drug development. The role of scientific and technical expertise is not limited just to the discovery of new drug candidates, however; it is also critical for identifying appropriate disease opportunities for any new discoveries, defining successful regulatory pathways to approval, and designing effective clinical trial strategies that will satisfy the FDA.

As knowledge of the pathophysiology of disease became more complex, so too did the clinical trial designs that were required to prove efficacy and safety. And as the number of new therapeutic areas under exploration continued to grow, expertise in the nuances of treating the disease of interest as well as in regulatory study design became essential for successful clinical trial management. The importance of practical experience in clinical trial design cannot be overemphasized if a company is to successfully navigate the gauntlet of scientific, medical, statistical, legal, and regulatory requirements that must be met in order to generate the data that will convince the FDA to approve a new therapeutic molecule. Computers have accelerated and dramatically enhanced the drug development process by making it possible to analyze larger sets of data using any number of variables, while recent innovations in information technology have increased the utility of software-based laboratory and medical instrumentation, which have only added to clinical trial expectations. Unfortunately, only a limited number of clinical trial experts is available with the experience to design the comprehensive protocols required for disease-specific trials that will satisfy the criteria for both regulatory approval and commercial success. Furthermore, as the number of patients required for these trials has increased, it has become necessary to expand clinical trials into international markets, necessitating another level of regulatory and clinical trial expertise.

For years, the available pool of scientific talent in the industry delivered breakthrough products unequaled since the discovery of penicillin. The robust successes of the 1980s and 1990s, however, spawned a critical mass mentality (i.e., that increasing the scale of R&D would increase the probability of success). Senior management also believed that a larger investment in drug discovery resources would ultimately lead to more drug candidates with a broader range of therapeutic indications. At the same time, they concluded that increasing the size of clinical development teams would speed up the clinical trials process and accelerate the filing of New Drug Applications.

Healthy revenue streams and high profit margins provided seemingly limitless funding for research. The industry made huge investments in facilities, new technologies, and scientific talent. Companies continued to broaden their therapeutic areas of interest and tried to increase their chances of success with a "more shots on goal" approach to drug development (i.e., the more products in development, the better the chances that some of them would make it through the FDA approval process). Along with more therapeutic areas and more products came a commensurate need for additional research expertise. But, when several companies pursue drugs in the same therapeutic area with the same molecular process or target or mechanism of action, the available supply of scientific and medical expertise, competence, and proficiency is quickly depleted, leading to a dilution of relevant scientific talent across the industry.

As in most professions, expertise and competence in pharmaceutical research are not always transferable. Expertise in chemistry-derived products (small molecules) differs from expertise in protein-based products (large molecules). Similarly, the science and technology behind cardiovascular diseases, for example, do not necessarily transfer to cancer or neurological disorders. At the same time, rapid increases in organizational size led to a further dilution of drug development expertise within companies and across larger, less focused, bureaucratically-managed pharmaceutical company research organizations. This growth in the scale of research produced the opposite of the intended effect (an unintended consequence) and created an expensive, inefficient, and less productive R&D environment that still exists within many pharmaceutical companies today. More therapeutic categories were explored, placing a strain on the few individuals with the necessary expertise within companies and across the industry. This created a situation in which researchers with limited expertise were forced to take on projects and programs they were not yet ready to manage. Another unintended consequence of this growth in R&D was that the best researchers from one therapeutic area were often promoted to direct programs in other therapeutic areas, which ironically led to a dilution of expertise in both areas.

Some companies also found that their in-house scientific operations had become obsolete by virtue of shifts in the company's strategy. For example, companies that shifted from antibiotic research to oncology were left with a huge infrastructure to support antibiotic discovery and development which had little applicability to the new therapeutic area of interest. Organizations that were unwilling to acknowledge the obsolescence this revision in organizational research strategy created often did not have the discipline to eliminate the now non-core programs. Underperforming departments and pet projects continued to drain valuable resources from priority programs for years. More often than not, even when pet projects were eliminated, hundreds of scientists with old-strategy expertise were compassionately reassigned to the new areas of focus where they began to learn the science but contributed only marginally to drug development.

With increasing organizational growth and massive R&D budgets, the complexities of managing these larger organizations helped create environments that were no longer conducive to innovative research. This resulted in less rigorous R&D project evaluation and prioritization (portfolio management), more consensus decision-making by committee, meaningless timeline discipline, and a diffusion in accountability. Key members of the scientific staff also had to decide, often on a daily basis, whether to apply their expertise to research projects or attend to administrative tasks. Even those researchers who successfully made the shift to management struggled to keep up with administrative duties (e.g., meetings, presentations, report preparation, and paperwork processing). Management oversight of research projects and budget details became increasingly superficial and often politically divisive as research managers lobbied for more funding to ensure their fair share of the research budget, regardless of the value of their projects to the financial health of the company. The list of ongoing research projects and programs grew in response to the "more-shots-on-goal" mentality and the lack of discipline in research portfolio assessments. Press releases and financial analyst discussions often highlighted the number of programs and compounds in the pipeline. Promising results from a few programs often overshadowed poor results and lack of progress for others. Underperforming programs were rarely eliminated. The imposition of template-structured development plans (i.e., trying to fit all research tasks and projects into a standardized project management format), administrative duties, and seemingly meaningless but irritating budget planning processes became especially challenging for scientific researchers who just wanted to find cures for disease. Those with specialized expertise often became lost in the bureaucratic maze of researchers, laboratory technicians, and inexperienced managers.

The dilution of scientific and drug development expertise had significant financial and market consequences for companies and for the industry. The single biggest impact of diminished research expertise was fewer truly innovative products—with meaningful clinical differentiation from other therapeutic options—and a reduction in productivity resulting from:

1. An over-reliance on computer-assisted drug design, molecular modeling, and high-throughput screening to identify potential drug candidates;
2. Inexperienced research managers attempting to manage too many people, leaving less time for rigorous oversight and scientific guidance on research projects;
3. Less rigorous portfolio management (research pipeline projects) including:
    - Managing too many projects;
    - Having too many projects with a low probability of success and low commercial potential;
    - Having too many basic science research projects that are unrelated to the drug discovery interests of the company and with limited potential to produce viable drug candidates;
4. Misguided and inappropriate project plans including:
    - Unnecessary testing and inconclusive studies;
    - Unrealistic timelines and budgets;
    - Plans that will fail to deliver the prerequisite data for FDA approval;
5. Applying the wrong research tools and techniques;
6. An inability to correctly interpret test results;
7. An inability to extrapolate research findings beyond the therapeutic focus of the ongoing program;

8. An inability to decide when to terminate a project;
9. Assigning priority to the speed of drug development over fully understanding the science behind the drug candidate, which results in prematurely advancing (with-out sufficient scientific basis) drug candidates to the next stage of development; and
10. Aligning incentive compensation with timelines and project milestones, thereby compromising drug development decisions and prematurely moving projects forward.

As a practical matter, some of these problems also contributed to the high failure rate of products in late-stage clinical development (Phase III). In 2004, former FDA commissioner Lester Crawford, addressing the PhRMA annual meeting, noted that almost 50% of new drug applications failed in Phase III clinical trials. He also noted the lack of success in extrapolating information gleaned from basic science research to the clinic.[1]

Driven by the need for good news and the expectations of Wall Street for pipeline progress, there is intense organizational pressure to move projects through the drug development process. Late-stage clinical failures often result from a lack of research expertise, poor management oversight, and the decision to move pipeline projects and programs forward prematurely. Allowing research projects that should be terminated to advance can also result from a lack of understanding of the basic science behind a drug candidate, design flaws that overlook or misrepresent preclinical toxicities, exaggerating marginal efficacy in early clinical studies, or minimizing clinical toxicity data.

The Pharmaceutical Research Manufacturers of America often cites the industry's poor R&D record as proof of the difficulty of finding good drug candidates and the risks of drug development. They frequently remind the public that "for every 10,000 compounds investigated, only five are ever tested as potential medicines in a clinical trial. Of those five, only one is ever approved for patient use."[2] While these numbers may describe the historical track record, it is more likely that they reflect poor R&D performance, diminished expertise, unmanageable organizational size, and a focus on pushing drugs through development, rather than the oft-cited risks and high costs of creating innovative new drugs.

When combined with poor management oversight, a lack of expertise can also lead to wasteful spending and pipeline expansions of programs with little or no commercial potential. Established programs become more difficult to eliminate; the farther along the clinical development path, the more press and other media coverage a drug candidate receives and the higher the expectations of success (interested readers should read the press releases and other articles about the projected revenue stream for Exubera®, estimated at over $1 billion a year*).[3] Because the costs of drug development rise dramatically at each stage of drug development, programs that should be terminated but continue to move forward drain valuable resources, including expertise, from other more deserving programs. Some companies eventually recognized this resource drain and began to adopt a "kill projects sooner rather than later" approach to pipeline projects. While this may represent a good strategy for compounds that have undergone sufficient preclinical testing, it may result in premature termination of products with unexplored applications in different therapeutic areas than those initially studied.

Despite progressively diminishing product innovation, the pipeline successes of the 1970s through the 1990s also created an industry research climate best exemplified by the "not-invented-here" mentality. For years, smaller companies with promising technologies and products found it nearly impossible to spark the interest of large pharmaceutical company research departments. Business development executives at Big Pharma relied on their own research teams to evaluate in-licensing opportunities and, as might be expected, these researchers either did not have the expertise to understand the innovative new technologies or perhaps felt threatened by them. One can only speculate as to how many creative new products the industry turned down as a result of this arrogance.

* A recent example of the hype that often surrounds a new drug candidate is Pfizer's ill-fated attempt to market Exubera®, an inhaled form of insulin developed in conjunction with Nektar Therapeutics, a California-based biotechnology company. Just days before receiving FDA approval in January 2006, Pfizer purchased the worldwide rights to inhaled human insulin from Sanofi-Aventis for $1.3 billion. After it became clear that there were too many hurdles to overcome to achieve market acceptance, Pfizer pulled the plug on the drug in October 2007 after less than two years. In one of the biggest pharmaceutical debacles in modern history, the company reported sales of only $12 million in the first nine months of 2007 after predicting annual sales of over $1 billion! The company took a write-off of $2.8 billion for costs associated with the drug.

For more than twenty years, pharmaceutical companies, with few exceptions (e.g., Eli Lilly, Bayer), ignored the potential of large molecule therapeutic agents either because they lacked the expertise, did not believe in their therapeutic value, or, more likely, felt they could make analogous small molecule alternatives using traditional synthetic chemistry. Today, pharmaceutical companies can no longer ignore the value of genomics and proteomics, especially considering their potential to deliver personalized medicine. The technologies available to explore these fields have the capacity to produce drugs and diagnostics that are specifically designed for a patient's genotype or genetic make-up. However, personalized molecular medicine will require very different expertise, including molecular biology and diagnostic device development, which is not readily available at most pharmaceutical companies. Additionally, industry-wide interest in exploiting these new technologies will lead to a further dilution of available expertise (which currently resides mostly in biotechnology companies) across the industry.

One of the unexpected and perhaps surprising consequences of diminished research expertise throughout the industry was the apparent disregard and willful compromise of scientific integrity. Litigation, congressional hearings, and whistleblower cases forced uncomfortable, embarrassing public disclosures of scientific indiscretions. These misdeeds included alleged and proven cases of scientifically downplaying potentially fatal side effects, selective and manipulative disclosure of clinical data, covering up clinical trial fraud, ghostwriting of scientific publications,* and support of off-label promotion. Considering that the industry's credibility is

* Companies often hire outside medical writers (ghostwriters) at considerable expense (often through their advertising agencies) to create publications based on company-funded studies, because the investigators who carried out the studies either do not have the time to write or because they lack good writing skills. These writers are then coached by the company or advertising agency as to what to emphasize (and what to omit) in the report. Companies often rely on the cozy relationships they have with investigators to persuade them to approve content. Only after the company has put its imprimatur on the paper will it be submitted to a journal for publication. In the past, disclosures were rarely made in the paper about either the ghostwriting or the control that companies exerted with regard to content, but most journals now require full disclosure statements from authors.

highly dependent on rigorous science and full and accurate disclosure, this blatant and seemingly widespread disregard for scientific and corporate integrity is shocking and disconcerting.

In an earlier chapter, we discussed the cases involving Neurontin® and Ketek® in which questionable scientific integrity and lack of disclosure put some patients at risk. Another more recent case started with an investigation of the cardiovascular side effects allegedly caused by Vioxx® (rofecoxib), a Cox-2 inhibitor indicated for the treatment of osteoarthritis and acute and chronic pain.* The drug, which was marketed by Merck, received FDA approval in 1999 and was subsequently removed from the market in 2004. Even after a landmark clinical trial involving more than 8000 patients (nicknamed VIGOR for Vioxx GI Outcomes Research) that was published in November 2000 in the *New England Journal of Medicine* suggested a possibly higher rate of heart attack in the Vioxx group than in the naproxen (another non-steroidal anti-inflammatory drug marketed under a variety of trade names) group,[4] Merck was slow to acknowledge that there might be a problem. This reluctance was understandable given that sales of Vioxx were booming ($2.5 billion in 2003),[5] with estimates that as many as two million patients in the United States were taking the drug at the time of its withdrawal and that 84 million people worldwide had taken the drug since its approval.[6]

Independent researchers who reevaluated the original trial data and the results of subsequent trials continued to raise concerns about the drug's safety.[7,8] A subsequent study sponsored by Merck revealed that there was indeed a greater risk of adverse cardiovascular events, including heart attacks and stroke, in patients who took the drug for more than eighteen months.[9] Internal Merck documents later revealed that management seemed to dismiss the concerns of experts and intentionally downplayed the possible dangers associated with Vioxx®. These documents also revealed that Merck trained their sales reps to sell through the safety issues and concerns using company-prepared cardiovascular cards that were found to contain misleading safety information.[10]

* Cox-2, or cyclooxygenase inhibitors, are drugs such as rofecoxib that block the Cox-2 enzyme. Blocking this enzyme inhibits the formation of prostaglandins (a type of chemical messenger) that are responsible for the pain and swelling associated with inflammatory diseases such as arthritis. These drugs are also referred to as non-steroidal anti-inflammatory drugs (NSAIDs).

Although Merck eventually agreed to establish a $4.85 billion fund to resolve thousands of injury claims,[11] many plaintiffs continued to allege that Merck knew about the risk of adverse cardiovascular events, intentionally under-reported that risk in company literature, continued to promote the product without warning physicians and patients about the risk, and made public statements that down-played the risks associated with the drug.

The above case is just one of many in which companies defended their continued product promotion and the exposure of patients to unsafe drugs in light of scientific data suggesting there could be potentially fatal consequences. These cases highlight the need for personal, scientific, and corporate integrity. The resulting unchecked mistakes and poor decisions underscore the problems associated with organizational growth and the resulting dilution of available scientific and research managerial expertise. In most instances, growth exceeded management's ability to apply the expertise they had and to provide the guidance, discipline, and oversight necessary to ensure the productivity and integrity of their operations. Arrogance and public denials made during the resulting product liability cases contributed greatly to the now-tarnished image and reduced credibility of pharmaceutical industry research and to the public's perception of the industry as biased and self-serving.

Despite more than $65 billion in annual R&D spending, the pharmaceutical industry has little of promise in its depleted pipelines. As long as the industry expects to command premium prices for its products, the market will increasingly expect those products to demonstrate their advantages over currently available treatment options. As more blockbuster drugs come off patent, companies will be forced to prove that their products are more effective or safer than generic alternatives. This need to demonstrate value and greater comparative efficacy has significant implications for pharmaceutical R&D. Merely discovering new compounds that are safe and effective is no longer sufficient to ensure commercial viability or success. In order to meet the market's expectations and command profitable premium pricing, companies will need to invest in finding cures and, more importantly, broaden the value-added benefits to include companion diagnostic tests to validate and support the appropriate use of new products. These diagnostic tests will be expected to identify appropriate patient candidates (high-probability responders), exclude patients who are likely to experience adverse reactions to the new treatment, and determine whether or not the treatment is working. These market expectations will require companies to build multidisciplinary R&D teams with expertise that extends well beyond the traditional drug discovery and development resources currently in place. Companies that embrace these changes should be able to deliver innovative new products that are safe and effective when used in the right patients while commanding premium prices that deliver sustainable revenues and long-term profits.

Chapter 12

So What Really Goes on in the Executive Suite?

The everyday work lives of pharmaceutical executives (C-level executives, general counsel, and corporate officers), like those of the executives of most large publicly traded companies, are completely disconnected from the experiences of their average workers and the customers the company serves. In an effort to maximize the use of their time, these individuals avoid menial tasks, and every conceivable convenience is afforded them. From scheduling their days to making travel arrangements to ensuring they have the right paperwork for every meeting to taking notes at meetings, well-paid executive assistants cater to their every need. Don't worry about lunch; it's already been scheduled for you and your guests in the executive dining room, where the executive chef on staff has prepared the menu to your liking. Have to get home early today so you can entertain some business associates tonight at a professional basketball game? No problem. The corporate helicopter will take you home so that you can stay longer at the office and still avoid the traffic. You can eat dinner at the suite during the game. And by the way, the corporate jet is scheduled to take you and the family to your industry conference in Phoenix this weekend where a tee time has been scheduled for you and your industry buddies after the meetings.

For most pharmaceutical industry executives, the perks are a part of the job which, in a global business, means 24/7 availability. Very quickly, the perks become highly addicting. The thrill of having a corporation and its assets at your disposal is intoxicating and, for many, a tremendous ego boost. And then there are the multimillion-dollar salaries, bonuses, and stock options, many of which continue into retirement, even if you are terminated.

Executives are provided with generous perks and compensation packages as inducements to stay with the company for as long as the Board of Directors wants them; shareholders have very little say over corporate officer tenure. In return, executives are expected to manage the company properly (i.e., to foster growth and prosperity) while avoiding liabilities that could damage the company or its image. So what were the highly paid pharmaceutical executives doing when their R&D programs were spending record amounts of money with little to show for these expenditures? Where were they when their companies were engaging in questionable and sometimes illegal activities? Did the healthy cash flow and personal perks blind them to what was going on? And even more importantly, where was the corporate legal counsel while these questionable and sometimes illegal activities were occurring? Like most large publicly traded companies, pharmaceutical companies have large legal staffs that are also supported by multi-million-dollar contracts with outside counsel from numerous law firms, each with its own area of expertise. Company lawyers are usually assigned to perform legal reviews of advertising and promotion campaigns to ensure compliance with legal as well as regulatory requirements. So just how do pharmaceutical companies engage in illegal activities when their executives and legal counsel are supposed to prevent this from happening in the first place?

Given the lack of a clear response to the serious problems that have been plaguing the industry over the past several decades, one has to wonder what executives, senior managers, and corporate legal counsels were doing while all of this was occurring. Were they unaware of their diminishing pipelines and declining R&D productivity? How could they be so disconnected from their own research programs that they didn't know about the potentially fatal side effects of the products they were marketing? How could they have been so blind to the types of egregious commercialization tactics discussed in previous chapters? Was this lack of intervention intentional, or was it due to poor decision-making, or lax management oversight, or all of these?

We have already discussed how sales and marketing organizations have served as a primary source of senior management talent. Progressively diminishing expertise in these areas led to a strain on the available pool of competent, well-trained, experienced senior managers and executives throughout the pharmaceutical industry. Again, despite the industry's best efforts with on-the-job and didactic management training, it could not keep up with the ever increasing demand for experienced executive leadership. While the industry does have some very talented executives, there are fewer than might be expected, considering that it employs nearly seven hundred thousand people in the United States alone[1] and spends millions of dollars on management training and executive development.

Perhaps one of the most telling examples of diminished management depth in the industry occurred in 1994 when Raymond Gilmartin, an industry outsider with an excellent eighteen-year record at Becton-Dickinson (a medical supply company),[2] was hired to replace Dr. Roy Vagelos as CEO of Merck & Co. For the first time in its history, the Merck Board of Directors ventured outside the company and even outside the industry to find the expertise it was looking for in its new CEO. This is not the only example of companies looking outside the industry for leadership. Prior to joining Pfizer in 2002 as Senior Vice President and General Counsel and subsequently being appointed CEO in 2006, Jeffrey Kindler held a number of executive positions at McDonald's Corporation including Chairman of Boston Market.[3] Mr. Kindler's ascent to the CEO position at Pfizer and the more recent appointment of Joseph Jimenez as CEO of Novartis in 2010 suggest that, for various reasons, pharmaceutical boards still feel a need to look beyond the industry for executive talent. Indeed, while Mr. Jimenez has considerable experience in consumer products businesses (H.J. Heinz Co., The Clorox Co., ConAgra Foods), his pharmaceutical industry experience is limited (he was a non-executive Board member at AstraZeneca and spent two years as CEO of the largest pharmaceutical business at Novartis).[4]

While it is encouraging that the industry can attract outside talent, which may offer fresh perspectives, it is disappointing that industry management development programs have failed to adequately prepare in-house candidates for these important roles. The cascading effects of depleted expertise across the industry at the executive level can have far greater implications than reduced expertise at any other organizational level and may include:

- Fewer experienced role models and less effective mentoring;
- Less insightful, less rigorous, and potentially flawed strategic planning that affects the entire business;
- Less attentive organizational oversight resulting in diminished operational accountability, wasteful spending, and lack of awareness about what is going on in the company;

- Increased vulnerability to regulatory and legal risks;
- Unrealistic or meaningless performance expectations resulting in progressively diminishing operational efficiency and a concomitant reduction in employee morale;
- An inability to recognize and correct mistakes and poor decisions made at lower levels in the organization;
- Publicly disclosed organizational missteps that perpetuate a market perception of executive incompetence; and
- A disconnect from market dynamics and the degree to which the company is meeting customer needs and expectations (think U.S. auto industry in the 1980s and 1990s).

Even today, the best pharmaceutical executives struggle with the challenges of managing large organizations in a complex and rapidly changing health care market. As mentioned previously, diligent management oversight is one of the first casualties to occur in large organizations as executives get caught up in administrative duties, answering queries from Wall Street analysts and journalists, spending time on the Boards of other companies, lobbying with policy makers, and schmoozing with their own Board of Directors (think incentive compensation here). Unfortunately, these distractions interfere with their ability to provide guidance on everything from strategy formulation and goal-setting to operational performance expectations. As a result, these executives rely heavily on their management teams (often with limited experience) for business planning, operational reviews, and due diligence oversight. This author believes that the lack of experienced managerial oversight represents one of the main reasons for the pharmaceutical industry's current difficulties.

Perhaps the least appreciated benefit of diligent management oversight is establishing and maintaining a corporate culture of integrity. One of the liabilities of a lack of oversight is the potential for organizational misconduct ranging from trivial falsification of expense reports and wasteful spending to serious regulatory and/or legal issues. Frequent oversight and timely interventions should preclude any individual or group of individuals from engaging in conduct detrimental to the company. Judging from disclosure of the types of industry improprieties discussed earlier, pharmaceutical company executives were either asleep at the switch, totally disconnected from their organizations, misled by their management teams, intentionally unaware, or, worse yet, complicit in the questionable behaviors described in this book.

Decades of litigation and legal discovery have uncovered numerous internal pharmaceutical company files that document the apparent intentional disregard for regulatory compliance, repeated cases of scientific misconduct, lack of full disclosure about serious adverse events, and a willingness to put patient safety at risk to increase or protect product sales. Incompetence, arrogance, lack of integrity, and ignorance (due to poor management oversight) are the only possible explanations for the claims of innocence by pharmaceutical executives in these publicly adjudicated cases. And yet, despite the highly visible and seemingly endless stream of litigation against pharmaceutical companies, few company executives have been told by the FDA that they cannot work for or provide services to the pharmaceutical industry; few have paid personal fines or spent any time in jail, even for the most egregious offenses. Pleas of ignorance, well-scripted, well-rehearsed answers during legal depositions, token (in the context of revenues) financial settlements, and indemnity clauses have kept executives (especially at the C level) insulated from any personal consequences resulting from corporate misconduct. Indeed, few if any C-level executives have stepped forward to either defend or help exonerate those on the front lines who have been accused of illegal activities that, in many cases, they were instructed or cajoled to carry out on behalf of the company. And because these activities typically led to higher revenues and operating margins that enhanced the personal wealth of executives, there was little incentive (other than personal integrity) for those executives to intervene. In the end, perhaps these were nothing more than calculated decisions based on an assessment of risk versus reward. Clearly, the chances of getting caught were low. Personal liability was rarely an issue, especially for executives, while the revenue opportunities were almost too good to pass up, particularly in light of the relatively small fines and punitive damages awarded. If the types of illegal activities described in this book were approved because the downside risk was limited, then the public has nothing to rely on but the personal integrity of pharmaceutical company executives and corporate responsibility. The FDA and the justice system apparently do not wield a big enough stick.

While some industry executives may challenge the author's premise that their companies are too large and complex to manage properly, their pleas of ignorance about the numerous cases of fraud, falsification of data, illegal off-label promotion, and intentional withholding of safety data speak for themselves. Perhaps it is time for industry executives to take a page out of the new General Motors playbook and finally admit that they have greatly disappointed the public and are taking the necessary steps to ensure that these activities will no longer be tolerated in the future. This is unlikely to occur, however, until C-level executives take personal responsibility for the actions of their companies. Depending on the seriousness of the infraction, executives should forfeit compensation, tender their resignations, forego golden parachutes, and possibly even spend time in jail when their companies are found guilty of regulatory or legal misdeeds that should have been prevented.

Unfortunately, the industry's track record provides little hope that it can police itself and right the ship. Few in the healthcare market, including patients, now believe that pharmaceutical companies will be able to deliver the innovative lifesaving products that are desperately needed at a reasonable cost, or that marketers can be trusted to promote their products appropriately and honestly. As a result, more restrictions will likely be imposed on commercialization tactics, thus further limiting market awareness of branded proprietary prescription drugs. This may mean that fewer providers will know about these drugs and even fewer patients will have access to them.

Today more than ever, a tremendous need exists for expertise and integrity in the executive suites of pharmaceutical companies (and other companies as well). This leadership must have the courage to initiate the dramatic changes necessary to align their companies with the needs of the evolving new healthcare market. Experienced management oversight with timely interventions can enhance productivity in R&D, dramatically improve operational performance, and mitigate mistakes and poor decisions. Pharmaceutical executives who fail to embrace this new paradigm will find themselves in an uphill battle against a less tolerant market that will continue to avoid companies that cling to an outdated business model.

Chapter 13

Market Expectations and Realities

In response to the pharmaceutical industry's over-the-top antics, healthcare organizations, consumer advocacy groups, Congress, and even state legislatures have proposed their own fixes. With an initial focus on marketing and sales activities, the market is already imposing rules that restrict the way the industry does business. In order to prosper in the evolving new healthcare market, the industry must address four major concerns:

1. Direct or indirect payments to healthcare providers (including investigators, consultants, and advisors) by the pharmaceutical industry create potential conflicts of interest and compromise the healthcare provider's credibility;
2. Pharmaceutical companies can't be trusted to fund clinical research because the studies they fund are "designed to succeed," and the investigators who carry out the studies are biased to deliver a favorable outcome;
3. Industry-sponsored continuing medical education (referred to as CME in the industry) is not credible, and the industry should have no role in educating healthcare professionals about new drugs or new uses for existing products; and
4. Pharmaceutical companies should discover and develop innovative new products that are superior to currently available treatment options, and these products should be relatively inexpensive (comparable to the lowest prices available globally or priced similarly to generic products in the same therapeutic category).

While the industry has no one to blame but itself for fostering these concerns and for the backlash against it, reformers need to be careful not to permanently cripple a system that is currently the only viable option for developing and commercializing the yet to be discovered disease-conquering lifesaving drugs that all of us will need at some point in our lives.

The premise underlying the market's current mindset is that pharmaceutical companies cannot be trusted and that the scientists and clinicians who either work in or serve as consultants to the industry may not be credible sources of drug information. Those who want to eliminate pharmaceutical company influence argue that to ensure complete autonomy and to avoid any appearance of impropriety, no financial dealings should be permitted between companies and healthcare providers and their institutions. Industry critics also argue that the FDA review and approval process should be completely independent and that only those experts who have never received any financial support from the industry can be considered unbiased sources. Given this mindset, any researcher or clinical investigator who was ever paid for his or her work on preclinical or clinical studies, including studies carried out to support regulatory filings for a drug, could not be considered an unbiased credible source. While this position may seem Draconian, it is at the core of recent actions taken with regard to pharmaceutical company funding of CME programs, and it provides the rationale behind financial disclosure requirements and even accusations that the FDA is beholden to the industry because of user fees.[1]*

One of the assumptions of the above scenario is that clinical trials for new drugs should be carried out by independent clinical trials companies† or medical schools, which would be responsible for completion of all regulatory requirements for FDA approval. The more recent expectation for comparative efficacy studies should also be satisfied by these independent parties. Funding for clinical trials would come from the government or from pooled industry sources, similar to the user fees levied by the FDA. There would be an expectation of total transparency; all new informa-

* The Prescription Drug User Fee Act, which was passed in 1992, authorizes the FDA to collect various user fees from pharmaceutical companies. These fees currently account for approximately half of the FDA's budget for drug reviews.[2]

† Pharmaceutical companies often contract with outside companies called contract research organizations (CROs) that specialize in planning, designing, and implementing clinical trials. These companies also recruit physicians who enroll patients in the trial. Clinical trials can involve as few as 10-15 patients in Phase 0 or tens of thousands in Phase III or IV and cost tens of millions of dollars to complete.

tion including lab notebook data generated by the pharmaceutical company (mostly from preclinical studies) and data from clinical trials would be entered into an electronic data repository widely available to the public for analysis and interpretation, similar to the electronic availability of the human genome project. Only independent (uncompensated) interpretations of the raw data would be considered credible for presentation or publication. Once a pharmaceutical company believed there was sufficient data to seek approval, it could submit a request to the FDA for a review for approval. The FDA would then carry out its own independent analysis and interpretation of the available data. Any advisors to the FDA could not have participated in the preclinical or clinical trials nor could they have ever received money from a pharmaceutical company. If the product was approved, the pharmaceutical company could commercialize it but could only use FDA-approved product information or published data that was consistent with the approved indications (theoretically, the regulatory expectation today). To ensure regulatory compliance and avoid introducing new fabricated benefits, companies could not mine the public data warehouse to make claims other than those approved by the FDA.

At first glance, these measures may seem like a perfectly reasonable system to keep drug information from being tainted by pharmaceutical company influence. However, these proposals would also eliminate pharmaceutical company control over the process, the net effect of which would be to dampen industry and investor interest in drug discovery and development. The notion that a company would rely on a completely independent group to control the drug development process in the hope that after a ten-year period and a billion-dollar investment the company might receive FDA approval for one or more commercially viable indications is neither practical nor realistic. Besides the obvious loss of control, industry critics often fail to consider the following issues:

1. What entity is going to coordinate drug development studies? Will it be the Food and Drug Administration, the National Institutes of Health, a new government agency, regional academic centers (which are not without their own scientific indiscretions), or a yet to be established non-profit company? While some CROs have the logistical expertise and capacity to do some of the work, they also have a profit incentive that would be considered a conflict

of interest with the potential for introducing bias (e.g., by proposing larger, more expensive studies, by prolonging study execution, or by emphasizing marginal efficacy in Phase II studies in an effort to carry out larger and more profitable Phase III studies). Critics also fail to appreciate the level of resources that would be required to replace the current global drug development infrastructure with a completely independent one. Those who suggest medical schools or government institutions for the task have little appreciation for or understanding of the logistical complexities and support resources required to execute clinical trials involving thousands of patients at hundreds of sites.

2. Drug development costs can vary dramatically depending on the breadth and types of indications being investigated and study design (e.g., the number of patients to be enrolled, the number of study sites, the numbers and types of endpoints, the technology required to determine the endpoints, and time to completion). Unlike FDA-imposed user fees, which do not pay for the entire cost of the drug approval process, this system would have no equitable way to apportion pooled clinical trial money to account for the cost of study design variability other than to send a bill to the company sponsoring the trial. With no control or input into the process, companies would be at the financial mercy of the clinical trial coordinating group.
3. How long can independent investigators remain unbiased if they are being paid for their work? If one avenue of drug development leads down a blind alley, wouldn't investigators have a financial incentive to redirect the research to another avenue of development (e.g., sildenafil, which was approved in 1998 as a treatment for erectile dysfunction, was originally studied by Pfizer researchers as a possible treatment for angina pectoris or chest pain associated with heart disease). Would this be an example of financial conflict of interest or would it be considered a good development decision? While investigators or institutions could be limited to one study per drug, such a policy would put a significant strain on the availability of qualified clinical investigators and sites.
4. What incentives would independent investigators or drug developers have to complete the development process

(sufficient for FDA approval) of a compound in a timely fashion? Wouldn't investigators who were dependent on funding have an incentive to prolong development trials? While incentives for timely completion could be built into any contract, there will always remain the possibility that investigators might be unduly influenced by bonus money rather than allowing science to drive the process.

5. What criteria would be used for prioritizing projects (one company's drug versus another), determining the sequence of indications to be studied (investigator's interest versus commercial viability), and allocating resources (which product gets done first at which institutions)?
6. Who takes responsibility for assuring that regulatory requirements for trial design and execution will be sufficient to ensure drug approval? Since clinical investigators would presumably be biased, who would defend the data or proposed label claims and package insert wording? Would the FDA have the necessary expertise and clinical experience across all therapeutic development projects to do all of the evaluations?
7. If a study is flawed (e.g., if a company spends $200 million only to find out later that the wrong endpoint was used or there was investigator fraud), who is accountable and who would pay for the mistake?
8. Who is responsible for product liability if the clinical studies are insufficient to identify a potential adverse event or if a safety issue is missed during the independently designed and executed studies? Could patients still sue the pharmaceutical company even though the company had no control over the development process and depended entirely on the independently developed data? Moreover, all data would be publicly available, so what would be the basis for any litigation?
9. If paid investigators are not considered credible sources of information, who will present the data at scientific meetings, submit them for publication, or act in an advisory capacity regarding recommendations for use of the product? Would independent, unpaid clinicians who interpret the raw data but have no clinical experience with the drug fill these roles?
10. What assurances would a pharmaceutical company have

that the regulatory studies would be designed to deliver the indications and necessary data to successfully market the drug so that they could recoup their investment? Also, what assurances would a pharmaceutical company have that the drug's full potential would be reflected in the clinical studies?

Despite these challenges, readers may feel that this approach to drug development could work. The reality, however, is that the loss of control over drug development and resulting loss of investor interest would probably be enough to sink many of the changes proposed by industry critics. This author believes that it should be possible to resolve most of these issues without going to such extremes. Increased transparency, standardization of investigator and advisory payments, comprehensive peer-reviewed data disclosure, uncompromised scientific integrity, and a genuine commitment to building stronger science around innovative new products are practical solutions that would go a long way toward reestablishing the public's trust in industry-sponsored research.

Another area of market concern that must be addressed is the elimination of industry influence on healthcare professionals as the industry seeks new ways to promote its products. While it is unrealistic to expect the industry not to promote its products, the industry must reevaluate *how* it does so. Increased regulatory requirements and legal enforcement are starting to rein in some of the more egregious sales and marketing tactics (e.g., inappropriate gifting, off-label promotion, false claims, and pricing fraud), and this can be expected to continue. Boring as it may be, drug promotion should be centered on FDA-approved claims. Pharmaceutical company researchers need to do a much better job of developing clinical data that support claims of superior efficacy versus other products in the same therapeutic category. The days of using marketing hype and sales to differentiate products will soon be over. But stronger science that supports product claims will make for more effective sales and marketing. If clinically meaningful differentiation is not possible, companies and their management teams should not be surprised when customers move to the least expensive therapeutic option. At the same time, the market should not expect pharmaceutical companies with legitimate product claims to not promote those claims.

The ongoing lack of transparency with regard to payments to healthcare professionals and the dissemination of biased product information under the guise of education are also areas in desperate need of reform. The industry has historically used a wide variety of media to promote and educate the market. Unfortunately, companies have blurred the line between promotion and education. Indeed, most medical journals, conventions, seminars, and other venues including the Internet have been infiltrated and heavily subsidized by the industry. One solution being explored is for medical organizations, medical schools, physicians, and other healthcare providers to pick up the slack by sponsoring educational programs at their own expense. To date, however, none has demonstrated a willingness to do so to the extent the industry has in the past. On the contrary, as mentioned earlier, Stanford University School of Medicine, which previously made statements about the inappropriate financial influence of the pharmaceutical industry on medical education, recently accepted an unrestricted $3 million CME grant from Pfizer.[3,4]

While most industry critics may not believe it, some pharmaceutical sales and marketing programs have actually helped healthcare providers remain current with drug information and treatment options, and millions of patients are being treated who otherwise might not have even sought treatment. If one assumes that pharmaceutical sales and marketing will have a much more limited role in the evolving new healthcare market, two issues will need to be addressed with regard to educating the medical profession about new drug therapies. Replacing more than a billion dollars the industry spends annually on medical educational initiatives is perhaps the easiest one to address. Industry financial support represents about half the total amount (about $2.4 billion) currently spent on continuing medical education every year.[5] To make up for this shortfall, medical school subsidies, professional society dues, subscription fees, continuing medical education course fees, and conference admission fees would have to be increased substantially to fill the financial gap.

The other problem is how to disseminate information about the benefits versus the risks of prescription drugs, especially new drugs, to healthcare providers, without the influence of pharmaceutical companies. Again, this would require a substantial commitment from medical schools and their faculties, independent CME organizations, and professional organizations and societies. These groups would have to develop drug information independently, publish more independent CME-accredited articles, and present more training programs to replace the hundreds of industry-sponsored programs typically offered each year. One solution to ensuring independence and lack of bias would be to require that none of the speakers on these programs or authors of publications could have received any payments—either direct or indirect—from a pharmaceutical company involved in the therapeutic category being addressed in the program. Unfortunately, the limited number of expert presenters who have never received any payments from pharmaceutical companies and the sheer magnitude of the amount of medical education required annually make this proposition impractical. Thus, the goal of supplying healthcare providers with comprehensive, unbiased information about new drugs that is completely devoid of industry sponsorship or support may not be achievable at the present time.

The solution to this medical education dilemma is simple: the industry must reestablish itself as a trusted, credible source of information, and healthcare professionals must reduce their financial dependence on the industry. Clear restrictions in conjunction with nominal customary speaking fees and a more transparent relationship between pharmaceutical companies and clinicians—one based on scientific integrity rather than financial influence—would go a long way toward solving this problem.

Another even more challenging problem that pharmaceutical companies need to address is the market's unrealistic expectation for an endless stream of innovative yet cheap drugs. To be sure, the industry has not done itself any favors with its outrageous prices, especially for new cancer therapies (Table 13-1), and by increasing the prices on branded products by an astounding 9.3% in anticipation of healthcare reform.[6] The reality, however, is that drug prices for innovative new pharmaceuticals may never be low enough to satisfy patients and insurers. Indeed, so-called legislative and healthcare industry experts who posit dramatic reductions in healthcare costs as a result of controlling prescription drug prices will be disappointed when they run the numbers. With prescription drugs now accounting for a mere 10% of healthcare costs, drug costs could be eliminated entirely without significantly affecting overall healthcare costs. In fact, more than 70% of prescriptions are already being filled with inexpensive (many for as little as $1.00 per week) generic drugs.[7] The industry must still do its part by increasing R&D productivity (more innovative products for less R&D spending), reducing bloated budgets and wasteful operational spending and, more importantly, pricing its drugs fairly. But even under the best of circumstances, the market's expectation for innovative new drugs at generic drug prices is simply unrealistic. Indeed, one has to wonder how long generic drug companies will be able to sustain their razor-thin margins going forward in an increasingly demanding market.

While the industry must reestablish a strong foundation of scientific integrity around product information, engage in respon-

Table 13-1. The high cost of new cancer treatments

Drug	FDA Approval	Manufacturer	Disease	Approximate Cost
Provenge® vaccine	April 2010	Dendreon	Advanced prostate cancer	$93,000/ three infusions
Folotyn®	September 2009	Allos Therapeutics	Peripheral T-cell lymphoma	$30,000/ month
Arzerra®	October 2009	GlaxoSmith-Kline	Chronic lymphocytic leukemia	$98,000*
Rituxan®	February 2006	Genentech	Non-Hodgkin's lymphoma	$3,000/ month
Avastin®	February 2004	Genentech	Lung cancer	$2,750/ month†
Erbitux®	February 2004	Bristol-Myers Squibb	Colon cancer	$10,000/ month
Clolar®	December 2004	Genzyme	Childhood leukemia	$34,000/ week‡
Campath®	May 2001	Berlex	Chronic lymphocytic leukemia	$5,000/ week‡

* Six months of treatment
† Average monthly cost
‡ Drug is usually given for only a few weeks.

Sources:
Dendreon: Provenge to cost $93K for full course of treatment. Posted April 29, 2010. www.fiercebiotech.com
Medicare formulary coverage for top-selling biologics. Nat Biotechnol 2009;27:1082-1084.
Questioning a $30,000-a-month cancer drug. NY Times, December 5, 2009. www.fiercebiotech.com

sible and ethical commercialization practices, and price its products fairly, at the same time the healthcare market must also face some unpleasant realities including the following:

Pharmaceutical R&D will cost more in the future and will be associated with much higher risks.

Research efforts will have to focus on meeting regulatory and market expectations for comparative efficacy by demonstrating that a new product is more effective and/or safer than existing products in the same therapeutic area. Drivers of the cost of meeting this goal will include the increasing costs associated with new technologies used in discovery research (including personnel), the number of clinical trials needed to definitively establish comparative efficacy superiority, the complexity of the trial designs, the number of patients needed, and the time it will take to complete clinical development and secure regulatory approval.

Discovery research (exploring biology and finding new patentable compounds) will take longer. Finding the innovative molecules will require pharmaceutical companies to renew their investment in the molecular and biochemical underpinnings of disease. In the evolving new environment, finding new pharmacologic targets and therapeutic compounds will require advanced new testing and assay procedures for identifying and screening drug candidates. To ensure success in late-stage development, more time and money will need to be spent to obtain a more comprehensive pharmacologic profile of early-stage drug candidates. While these investments in discovery expertise and technologies will generate more and potentially better product candidates, they will also require more aggressive intellectual property filings (think lawyers and patent prosecution filings). In fact, one of the biggest risks companies face is starting development on a drug candidate for which they have filed patent protection only to learn later (perhaps years later or after tens of millions of dollars have been spent on clinical trials) that a patent for a key ingredient or step in its manufacturing process has already been issued. Also, when several companies are focused on similar therapeutic areas and striving for superiority claims, the odds increase dramatically that they will be working on similar targets and molecules for which there can be only one winner, with comparative efficacy being the ultimate determining factor. While developing me-too drugs may have generated sufficient consolation (revenue) in the past, this strategy will no longer constitute a viable path to success in the evolving new healthcare market.

The recent legislative push for comparative effectiveness trials is a good example of changing market expectations that will force companies to design larger clinical trials than those whose only endpoints are proof of efficacy and safety.* The requirement to demonstrate comparative superiority will likely mean that thousands of additional patients will need to be enrolled in clinical trials, which will add considerable cost and several years to development timelines. The finite availability of researchers, clinical trial sites, and patients who are willing and qualified to participate in these trials will also add to the cost of research. Adding further to the cost will be the fees that researchers, clinicians, and patent attorneys with drug development expertise in certain therapeutic areas (e.g., oncology, autoimmune, and central nervous system diseases) will be able to command.

While some have argued that the expansion of personalized medicine (treatments tailored to individual patients) will help streamline clinical trials, this may not turn out to be the case since pharmaceutical companies, which are not known for their expertise in diagnostic testing development, will need to find partners who can discover and validate diagnostic tests to complement their treatment candidates. In order not to bias and complicate the analysis, clinical trials will be needed to first establish the drug's efficacy and safety, and then the diagnostic test will need to be studied with the drug to determine whether or not the new treatment has a personalized or simply a general treatment effect.

Against this backdrop, there is a real possibility that some companies may never market a compound that satisfies the regulatory requirements which will allow them to make a claim of superiority over existing treatments. Drug formularies that determine what products to include in their prescription drug plans will also require comparative efficacy data for all new products, especially those that have premium prices. The increasing costs of drug development and the distinct possibility that products may

* In the past, companies only had to prove that a new drug was safe and more effective than a placebo (an inert pill), or comparable to an approved drug. Now, in addition to gaining FDA approval, companies will have to demonstrate that a new drug is either more effective or safer than existing therapeutic options in order to be commercially successful.

never make it to market or be commercially viable will fundamentally change the risk-versus-reward investment profile of the pharmaceutical industry.

R&D will generate fewer marketable proprietary-branded products and fewer blockbuster products.

While pharmaceutical research has always been an expensive, high-risk endeavor, with effective marketing and sales campaigns even marginal products could generate substantial revenue. A small share of a large therapeutic market (e.g., cholesterol-lowering drugs) could provide significant returns and mitigate some of the risk, while the occasional blockbuster provided growth and attractive returns to investors. Unfortunately, in an era that produced many blockbuster drugs, most pharmaceutical companies spent hundreds of millions of dollars marketing me-too drugs. In the evolving new market, however, these marginal products will have little or no commercial value.

These challenges will result in fewer proprietary products making it to market, and higher-priced marginally better products will have essentially no chance of commercial success. While finding and developing a blockbuster product will still be possible, especially in certain therapeutic areas where there are tremendous unmet needs (e.g., cancer, disorders of the central nervous system, diabetes, etc.), such developments will be much less common than before. The market's expectations for and the willingness of third parties to pay for drugs with superior efficacy and safety will dictate how fast and to what extent a new product will gain entry into the market and ultimately how often the product is prescribed. On the other hand, finding and developing superior products that are priced according to their true value to patients will transform blockbuster drugs into super-blockbuster drugs as the market not only supports but encourages their use.

Because companies will need to focus on superior product profiles, new compounds that do not demonstrate significant potential early in development may be dropped prematurely. This is unfortunate, since the true therapeutic potential of many treatments does not become apparent until late in the clinical trials process or until after they have been on the market for a few years (e.g., most cancer drugs). In the future, companies will need more discovery product candidates with stronger profiles that better portray their potential for clinical superiority. This will be a much more difficult hurdle for most pharmaceutical companies, given the recent industry-wide drought in innovation.

In summary, companies can no longer afford to ignore the market's expectation for superior product profiles. The time required to discover and develop innovative new products (as much as 10 to 15 years) means that companies must immediately begin to change their approach to R&D, reevaluate their current projects, and recalibrate their business development (acquiring in-licensing technologies from outside the company) criteria in the context of this evolving market expectation. For some companies, this means cleaning out their current pipeline to a point where nothing may be left. Pharmaceutical companies that are not rigorous and disciplined in their pipeline assessments will be disappointed by the market's lack of enthusiasm for mediocre products and will face huge financial losses as well as diminished investor confidence and interest.

The industry must take the necessary steps to become a trusted, credible source of drug information.

As discussed earlier, a lack of industry credibility has fostered a demand for complete transparency in virtually everything the industry does. Tactics that undermine scientific and commercial integrity have made it difficult for the market to accept pharmaceutical companies as a credible source of drug information. *This must change.* At the same time, the evolving new healthcare market must acknowledge that pharmaceutical companies need to promote their products, compensate drug development investigators, and educate healthcare providers about new products, particularly since the industry currently represents the only viable option for drug development.

One way for the industry to address the market's need for credible drug information lies in designing rigorous clinical trials and making all data generated during the trials available to the public. New drugs that are based on good science along with market-sensitive commercialization tactics will go a long way toward helping to rebuild the industry's image and credibility. The recent agreement to curtail promotional CME, disclose financial payments to clinicians, and post clinical study data online are good first steps. But the industry needs to do more to gain the public's trust. At the heart of this distrust has been the lack of corporate, personal, and scientific integrity. If companies do not overhaul their flawed corporate cultures and engage in responsible behavior, the outlook is dismal. Breakthrough products marketed by companies that engage in tactics the market abhors will take longer to gain market acceptance, which means that fewer patients will benefit from them.

Market-imposed constraints on growth and profitability may lead to reduced investor interest in drug development.

Decades of outrageous commercialization tactics by the industry have created a backlash against the companies as part of an effort to reduce the cost of drug therapy. However, the punitive measures that are now being imposed and contemplated may become counter-productive if pharmaceutical companies and their investors conclude that the probability of success and return on investment no longer justify the cost and time required to develop innovative new drugs. This has already occurred with vaccines and antibiotics, although vaccine research has been reinvigorated by the recent H1N1 flu pandemic that led to large government purchases and subsidies for research. Similarly, increasingly challenging regulatory expectations, restricted new product use (including limited access to formularies and the need for prior approval from infectious diseases specialists for antibiotic prescriptions written by non-infectious-diseases physicians) as well as a reluctance by the market to pay for innovation have led to the development and commercialization of fewer new antibiotics, despite increasing concerns about hospital-related mortality resulting from highly resistant strains of gram-negative bacteria such as *Acinetobacter baumanii* and *Klebsiella pneumoniae* and gram-positive bacteria such as methicillin-resistant *Staphylococcus aureus* (referred to as MRSA).* Long development times, increased regulatory demands and market expectations, increasingly costly research, more constraints on commercialization, and the potential for product liability lawsuits all make pharmaceuticals a less attractive investment option. This is not a veiled threat from an industry insider but a reality for any business, including pharma-

* Gram-negative and gram-positive refer to the ability of bacteria to take up a type of stain called a Gram stain, which was invented in 1882 by a Danish bacteriologist by the name of Hans Christian Gram. Due to differences in their cell walls, gram-positive bacteria stain purple while gram-negative bacteria stain pink.

ceuticals. Investment in businesses is directly related to the risk assumed and the probability of a return on investment within a given time frame. Because of the inherent high risks associated with drug discovery and development, without the prospects for a higher than average return on investment within a reasonable time frame, investment interest will decline.

The industry must foster a renewed appreciation for the potential benefits of drug therapy in terms of reduced hospitalizations and serious medical events (e.g., stroke, heart attacks, etc.) and greater life expectancy.

The industry often bases its "what the market will bear" pricing strategies and market-insensitive price increases on unsubstantiated arguments such as the high risk and cost of R&D. Although the investment required for discovering and developing new drugs must be acknowledged, the industry needs more scientifically credible patient-friendly data to substantiate the value of innovative new treatments. One example would be the use of electronic medical records to quantify the financial impact of drug treatment by determining the cost savings from reduced medical events, fewer emergency room visits, and fewer hospitalizations.

Apart from discovering and developing new products that meet the market's expectations for superior clinical efficacy and safety over existing products, reestablishing trust and credibility with a skeptical public is the biggest challenge that pharmaceutical companies face in the evolving new healthcare market. Unfortunately, it will take years of good behavior (and not just empty proclamations and acts of philanthropy) that demonstrate a renewed commitment to patient care (rather than just profits) for the industry to dig itself out of the hole it has dug for itself. At the same time, there must be sufficient financial incentives for the industry to function and innovate. An oppressive healthcare market with unrealistic expectations will dampen investor enthusiasm, making it difficult for the industry to attract the necessary scientific expertise and, ultimately, decreasing the probability of producing a stream of innovative new products. Indeed, without the ability to earn a fair return on its investment, the industry and its investors will find little incentive to continue the search for the much-needed treatments that, as stated at the beginning of this chapter, all of us will need at some point in our lives.

Chapter 14

The Evolving New Healthcare Market

As suggested throughout this book, the healthcare market of the future will differ dramatically from that of the past. Every element of the traditional pharmaceutical industry business model will need to be reassessed in light of the market dynamics that will evolve over the next few decades. Although politicians have made numerous attempts to restructure the U.S. healthcare system in the past, a progressive administration and the unsustainable acceleration of healthcare costs have combined to make healthcare reform a high priority. Despite their rhetoric proclaiming a desire to work together to achieve a common goal, the various players in the system (insurance companies, hospitals, physicians, medical device companies, and the pharmaceutical industry) seem more concerned about protecting their financial interests than in participating in a constructive dialogue about how to control wildly escalating costs. Even though Congress has finally succeeded in passing a healthcare reform bill, it will take years before the full impact of the legislation is known. During this period, there will likely be considerable debate and legal challenges to many of the bill's provisions.

As expected, the pharmaceutical industry's response to healthcare reform has been to fight to protect its vested financial interests and manipulate policy to support its traditional business models and practices. And true to its nature, the industry has spent millions on lobbying and television ads designed to encourage reform while promising $80 billion in cost savings over ten years to garner White House support for protecting industry interests.[1] This gesture of support appears to have successfully preserved current industry business practices and fended off price controls, reimportation (purchasing cheaper drugs from foreign countries), and government price negotiations, at least for now.

Unfortunately, the appearance of cutting a deal behind closed doors infuriated legislators who were not involved in the process and reinforced the public's distrust of the industry. These actions also suggest that the industry does not view healthcare reform as a catalyst for change but rather as another business issue to be managed. Regardless of how healthcare reform plays out, the healthcare market is changing, and either healthcare reform or the rising cost of healthcare will simply accelerate the pace of change. So instead of continuing to conduct business as usual, industry leaders would be wise to listen to the "screaming market" and begin to formulate new strategies. Companies that are intent on maintaining traditional industry business practices or that decide to wait for clarity will be met with commercialization and product use restrictions that will lead to financial distress, regardless of the strength of the company's product line.

So what are some of the issues the market has identified and what role will they play in the evolving new market? Does anyone know exactly what this new market will look like? Perhaps not, but much can be learned from the market's dissatisfaction with the industry's past behavior and its expectations for the future. Perhaps more importantly, companies have a unique opportunity to reinvent themselves and create a competitive advantage in the midst of these changes. The following discussion can help companies assess their current state of readiness for the evolving market.

Healthcare reform

Considerable uncertainty persists about what healthcare reform will actually mean to providers and patients alike. This uncertainty includes how it will be implemented and how it will work. Healthcare reform appears to have two main goals: 1) to cover most Americans, regardless of their ability to pay, with some form of health insurance; and 2) to reduce and control the increase in healthcare costs. These two goals are interrelated in the sense that if the second goal is not achieved, providing healthcare for the millions of uninsured Americans will simply be unaffordable. In fact, one of the driving forces behind reform has been the unsustainable acceleration in healthcare costs (Figure 14-1), with total healthcare spending in the United States expected to reach $2.5 trillion in 2009,[2] an increase of 5.5% over 2008 and the largest one-year increase in healthcare's share of gross domestic product (GDP) in history.[3] This sum represents a whopping 17.6% of GDP

Figure 14-1. Total healthcare spending in the United States.

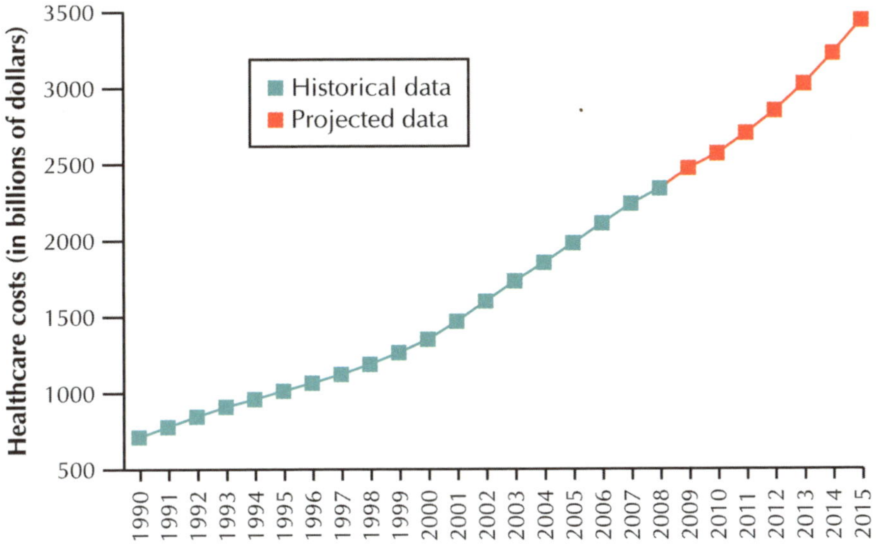

compared with less than 12% of GDP in other developed countries around the world.[4]

Regardless of how reform translates into practice, companies can anticipate several high-probability outcomes and begin to plan accordingly. The first is an intense focus on the cost of care. In order to provide healthcare for the millions of previously uninsured Americans, the market must manage down the cost of care and keep it in check. This will require rigorous expense oversight, intelligent use of health delivery resources, and an emphasis on providing affordable benefits to the majority rather than on Cadillac plans for the few. Identifying and implementing medical best practices and state-of-the-art electronic medical recordkeeping, reducing bureaucratic administrative costs, and using collective purchasing power are all expected to provide substantial cost savings.

Prescription drugs

Prescription drug use will increase dramatically in the evolving healthcare market as more patients are expected to have access to prescription drug coverage (at minimal or no cost), and drug treatment is utilized in an effort to reduce the incidence of hospitalizations and preventable, as well as more costly, medical events (e.g., heart attack, stroke). While generic drugs will be the dominant workhorses in this new market, cost containment pressures will make it increasingly difficult even for generic drug companies to remain profitable. In the evolving new market, proprietary branded pharmaceuticals will need to demonstrate clinical superiority over currently available products, including generic drugs that may not be chemically identical to the branded product but that have similar pharmacologic activity. There is already considerable medical support for developing evidence-based treatment guidelines and identifying best practice treatments that are supported by head-to-head clinical trials. The results of these trials will not only determine the relative value of new proprietary drugs but whether they will be included on formularies and covered by insurance plans. In addition to demonstrating clinical superiority over existing treatments, companies expecting to charge premium prices for innovative new products will have to provide credible real-world pharmacoeconomic (i.e., cost benefit) data that clearly demonstrate their value compared with less expensive treatments. Companies that market proprietary drugs without these data will find it difficult to win formulary committee approval and will face serious commercial challenges. Instead of trying to commercialize the umpteenth me-too drug, company executives ought to be asking themselves how many antihypertensive drugs or bisphosphonates or cholesterol-lowering agents or erectile dysfunction drugs or selective serotonin reuptake inhibitors a cost-conscious healthcare system will support.

One area that will provide significant opportunities for pharmaceutical companies in the evolving new market will be preventive medicine. Toward this end, it is likely that healthcare providers and insurers will aggressively promote a broad range of programs that encourage and support healthy lifestyle choices. Early diagnostic screenings, compliance with drug regimens, and routine vaccinations will become cost management tools rather than simply prudent things to do. And while considerable research needs to be carried out before patients derive benefit from companion diagnostics and personalized medicine (fitting the drug treatment to a individual's genetic or metabolic profile), their potential for cost savings will provide a strong incentive for their development (more about this later) and incorporation into drug treatment plans.

The drug commercialization process

Pharmaceutical sales and marketing will be affected more by changing market dynamics and restructuring than by regulatory compliance and enforcement actions. A less tolerant healthcare market in conjunction with more restrictive state and federal legislative rules will make most traditional sales and marketing tactics inefficient, ineffective, and obsolete. As the market becomes increasingly cost conscious, prescribing decisions will be influenced more by healthcare market bureaucrats and less by physicians. In fact, one of the biggest challenges facing pharmaceutical companies will be deciphering the multiple tiers of influence of a highly bureaucratic decision-making process. The complexity of the decision-making process combined with standardization of care using best practice treatments will undermine the impact of traditional sales and marketing tactics. Even if a decision-maker or point of influence is identified, the ability to influence product use will be limited and will be driven more by a rigorous review of published clinical data than by advertising and promotion. This process may involve several levels of review, committee consensus, and exacting formulary assessments. A strong preference for less expensive generic drugs will be extremely difficult to overcome. Ironically, truly superior drugs will not require the mass market approach and use of smoke-and-mirror commercialization tactics that often cost tens of millions of dollars to implement. Insurance plans and government programs will encourage and facilitate the use of appropriately priced superior products to maximize their treatment value.

For pharmaceutical sales and marketing campaigns to have any role in the evolving new healthcare market, they must fundamentally change while reestablishing trust and credibility. Companies that fail to understand or delay in making the necessary changes to their commercialization strategies and tactics will waste money and alienate the market they desperately seek to influence. In the end, they may find themselves with safe and effective drugs that have no market in the United States.

Pricing

We have already mentioned the expected dominance of generic drugs in the evolving new healthcare market. These drugs will be available at lower prices than ever before seen in the United

States. A market focus on cost containment, rigorous price negotiations with multiple suppliers, and the promise of large volumes never before imagined will force generic drug companies to sell their drugs at razor-thin profit margins. The multitude of high-quality generic drug suppliers will greatly reduce the ability of any one generic drug company to differentiate its products based on quality, service, and availability. As a result, smaller generic companies may find themselves being acquired by larger companies or withdrawing from the market completely. Some larger pharmaceutical companies with both branded and generic products will have to leverage their margin expectations across their entire product portfolio, perhaps selling their generic drugs at nominal or no profit.

For branded prescription drugs, pricing strategies will become increasingly complex for two major reasons. First, the government is already and will most likely continue to be one of the largest purchasers of prescription drugs. The requirement for "best price" concessions and the possibility (or threat) of the government obtaining legislative authority to negotiate prices directly with pharmaceutical companies underscore the importance of pricing and getting it right the first time. Regardless of the scenario, the push for transparency in the evolving new healthcare market could make government pricing the new benchmark at which all other price negotiations begin.

The second factor that will significantly affect pricing is the market's expectation and need for credible pharmacoeconomic data that support the use of all new prescription drugs, particularly those priced at a premium to other therapeutic options or those intended for smaller markets (e.g., orphan diseases). This means that companies will have to supply more clinical and actual real-world data to substantiate the value of a particular treatment compared with other therapeutic options. In theory, this should lead to more value-based pricing analyses and creative pricing strategies. Several companies (e.g., Johnson & Johnson, Merck, and Pfizer) are already exploring different pricing and reimbursement strategies including clinical outcome guarantees ("you don't pay unless the drug works"). At the same time, the value-pricing hurdle for innovative branded prescription drugs will be dramatically increased as simplistic cost-benefit analyses are compromised by the availability and use of cheaper therapeutically equivalent treatment options. With its focus on cost, the market will also be incentivized to challenge and marginalize traditional value metrics such as ease of use, quality of life, and the less objective, philosophical value of days or a few more weeks of life.

Even companies with strong clinical and economic data that support value-based pricing will face tough negotiations for plan inclusion and unrestricted use. Again, the pressure to control increases in healthcare costs will make prescription drugs an easy target for cost containment initiatives. In order to maintain reasonable profit margins in an increasingly cost-conscious environment, the industry will need to dramatically increase R&D productivity, significantly reduce operating expenses, and develop strong, irrefutable pharmacoeconomic data to support pricing strategies that are consistent with the market's expectation for value.

Global considerations

Although this book has focused primarily on the U.S. pharmaceutical market, the healthcare reform initiative may reignite a renewed global interest in the cost of prescription drugs. Pharmaceutical companies generally price their products based on local market conditions, so it should not be surprising that most countries, including many in Europe, Canada, and Latin America, benefit from lower prices than those in the United States.[5] Prices for drugs in emerging markets (e.g., China, Russia, and Brazil) are also typically lower than in the United States. With the U.S. healthcare market looking to reduce overall costs, lower global prices could become reference points that increase the pressure for reimportation of less expensive drugs back into the United States. This scenario poses a significant threat to profitability and value-based pricing strategies. If prescription drugs can be purchased from less expensive sources outside the United States, no amount of pharmacoeconomic data can overcome a lower price for the same product (even from the same manufacturer). Because the United States represents one of the largest and most profitable markets, protecting favorable prices in this country might lead pharmaceutical companies to consider adopting a single global pricing strategy. Unfortunately, such a strategy would lead to a significant loss of revenue and almost certainly mean that some medications would be priced out of the reach of most patients in developing countries. Regardless of how this plays out, the maintenance of lower international pricing builds an unrealistic expectation for similar low prices in the United States.

Slowing revenue growth

One of the most dramatic consequences of the evolving new healthcare market will be shrinking market opportunities and the reduced potential for revenue growth from proprietary branded pharmaceuticals. Despite an aging population and the fact that more patients have insurance coverage for prescription drugs, most patients will be treated with generic drugs. In anticipation of this change, some companies have started to develop or acquire generic drug businesses or are expanding into emerging markets to capture early-entry "low-hanging fruit." Most pharmaceutical companies, however, remain oblivious to the growth-limiting market realities of the evolving new healthcare market.

A number of factors will contribute to slowing revenue growth for the industry. The prospect of fewer blockbuster products that can meet the market's expectation for clinical superiority, the fact that several multi-billion-dollar blockbuster products will be coming off patent over the next few years, the increasingly dominant role of generic drugs, the ineffectiveness of traditional mass market commercialization tactics, and a limited ability to raise prices in an increasingly managed, highly cost-sensitive environment will all contribute to declining revenue growth. While opportunities to develop and market blockbuster drugs clearly exist, they will be fewer in number given the need to establish superiority over existing products. And if a new product does become the established best practice treatment of choice, it will become that much more difficult for other companies to enter that therapeutic market. Companies also need to understand that traditional commercialization tactics will no longer drive the sales of inferior or mediocre products; the companies will have limited access to and less influence on prescribers who will be bound by payers and insurers to use best practice treatments of choice.

Markets will become consolidated as the prospect of companion diagnostics and personalized medicine to identify those patients who are most likely to respond to treatment and those who might experience adverse reactions increasingly becomes a reality. Innovative new products that meet the market's expectations for superiority will produce healthy revenues and profits as they become widely used as standards of care, but in smaller patient populations. However, these products will be fewer in number (compared to me-too products) and will represent a smaller percentage of overall prescriptions written.

Impact on pharmaceutical research and development

The market's expectation for best practice treatments will drive pharmaceutical R&D in two ways. First, companies must find new methods to discover and develop truly innovative products with the potential to provide significant medical benefits over currently available therapeutic options. While decades of industry research have brought literally hundreds of new therapeutic agents to the market, few would pass the superior comparative therapeutic efficacy hurdle. While it may be relatively easy for a hospital or clinic to perform a loosely controlled comparative effectiveness study or a literature-based meta-analysis to determine which product to include in its best practice guidelines for a particular indication, the task of designing and executing these trials to the satisfaction of the FDA (which would allow the company to advertise the superiority of its product) is an altogether different matter. Indeed, designing clinical trials that establish a new product as the best treatment option for a particular indication will require large numbers of patients (tens of thousands for some therapeutic categories such as hypertension, hypercholesterolemia, or diabetes) in trials that evaluate various therapeutic options. One opportunity that precludes the need for superior efficacy is discovering and developing drugs and vaccines that prevent a disease in the first place. Compared to potential blockbusters, these projects have historically been difficult to justify in Big Pharma research portfolios. Financial assessment models often include penalties for the low probability of discovery success, unclear regulatory pathways, limited or lack of repeat business (no need for chronic treatment), and inherent liabilities (the patient becomes sick *after* taking the preventive treatment). However, this may change as the blockbuster model diminishes and the market looks to reduce overall healthcare costs.

Similarly, companion diagnostics and personalized medicine are attractive concepts for patients, healthcare providers, and payers alike (government and insurance companies). Identifying the right treatment for the right patient, only giving treatments that are needed, and avoiding treatments that produce serious side effects and adverse reactions in specific patients will all help to reduce cost. In order to deliver on this promise, however, diagnostic discovery and development expertise will need to become an integral part of pharmaceutical R&D. As mentioned earlier, companies will be expected to identify (using yet to be developed diagnostic tests and tools) which patients will respond favorably to drug treatment, which patients are actually responding to treatment, and which patients are likely to experience adverse reactions. At present, few pharmaceutical companies have the expertise to incorporate diagnostic discovery and development into their product development programs.

The regulatory environment

Few would argue that the FDA is not in need of serious reform. Several uncharacteristically embarrassing episodes of product approval and safety mishandlings have led to admonishment by Congress and diminished public trust in the agency. The FDA remains bureaucratic, inefficient, and underfunded. Symptoms of this chronic dysfunction include lengthy review backlogs, delinquent manufacturing facility inspections, and minimal punishment of even the most egregious marketing compliance misconduct. Given the renewed emphasis on healthcare reform, now would seem a perfect time for implementing the dramatic changes needed at the agency. The new FDA commissioner, Dr. Margaret Hamburg, has already indicated that more aggressive enforcement actions will be taken against companies that do not play by the rules, and she has acknowledged the need for additional expertise to expedite and improve the drug approval process.[6] Dismantling inefficient bureaucratic operations should clarify agency expectations, facilitate drug approvals (including generic drugs), and provide patients with confidence that the drugs they are taking are safe and effective and are being prescribed without misleading promotional influences from pharmaceutical companies. At the same time, companies can expect the FDA to be even more demanding in its expectation of integrity and transparency in medical and scientific research. Pharmaceutical marketing and sales teams can anticipate intensified surveillance and a higher compliance standard for advertising and promotional materials, thus forcing them to adhere to approved label claims, with less opportunity for embellishing nebulous features and unsubstantiated benefits of undifferentiated products. The agency will also be less tolerant of company-orchestrated off-label promotion campaigns that undermine the regulatory approval process.

Legal considerations

One possible outcome of healthcare reform may be a reduction in litigation against pharmaceutical companies. The market's demands for integrity, transparency, and disclosure, extensive due-diligence reviews by purchasing organizations and health insurance providers, regulatory constraints on commercialization, and an intense focus on product pricing should all contribute to fewer opportunities for regulatory and legal missteps on the part of the industry. A more comprehensive understanding of drugs and their possible toxicities along with comparative efficacy and pharmacoeconomic data will translate into substantially more clinical information being made available than ever before. This plethora of drug information in conjunction with comprehensive, transparent clinical trial data and severe restrictions on interactions between pharmaceutical companies and healthcare providers will make it increasingly difficult to support claims of negligence, misrepresentation, fraud, and non-disclosure. Ironically, it may be more difficult to hold companies responsible for inappropriate use of their products if they have limited access to healthcare providers (i.e., is a company liable for misuse of its products when it has minimal access to healthcare professionals?). Furthermore, restricted access may also expose healthcare providers and others to more litigation if they do not stay current with new treatment options and related prescribing information. To stay current and to avoid personal liability, healthcare providers and their employers will have to find credible and effective alternatives to information from sales representatives and industry-sponsored continuing medical education programs.

A sense of urgency

Companies must develop a sense of urgency in preparing for the market changes discussed in this chapter. In the evolving new healthcare market, successful companies will be proactive in enhancing their expertise and developing leadership and management teams. At the same time, they should be identifying the implications of these changes for their current business model and developing strategies for sustaining growth in an increasingly complex and challenging market. By its very nature, the pharmaceutical industry is slow to change, typically making incremental adjustments in response to systemic problems. Successful integrations of companies involved in mega-mergers has often taken decades; new products may take ten to fifteen years before they reach the market, and experienced leadership can also develop very slowly. If companies continue to wait for healthcare reform to roll out and the market to stabilize, they risk running out of time and cash as revenue streams decline, pricing pressures lead to lower profit margins, and R&D costs and drug development timelines increase. While considerable uncertainty remains about what healthcare reform will mean for the pharmaceutical industry, companies need to formulate plans and take action based on what they already know and can anticipate will occur. If industry executives truly get it, healthcare reform may actually turn out to be a blessing in disguise—one that helps define and shape an even more prosperous pharmaceutical industry of the future.

Chapter 15

Corporate Strategies and the Evolving New Healthcare Market

It now appears that the evolving new healthcare market will become increasingly standardized, and it will likely intensify its focus on cost control and budgetary compliance. Pharmaceutical companies involved in proprietary drug research will still strive to discover, develop, and commercialize innovative new products, but their emphasis will shift to developing drugs that will be accepted onto formularies and covered by prescription healthcare plans. In the best-case scenario, a new drug will be recognized as a best practice treatment for its approved therapeutic indication(s). Since formularies will strongly favor less expensive generic drugs, formulary approval and premium pricing will be reserved for innovative new products with documented cost benefits that are clinically superior to other treatment options.

While considerable uncertainly remains about what healthcare reform will mean in the long run, pharmaceutical companies are employing various near-term strategies to prepare for these changes. Some larger companies are using their cash reserves to become even bigger (e.g., Pfizer and Wyeth, Merck and Schering-Plough, Roche and Genentech). The rationale behind this mega-merger strategy is to realize near-term growth by combining revenues while enhancing profits by eliminating operational redundancies and excess infrastructure. The players who engineer these mega-mergers believe that, over the long term, market muscle and critical mass will help these very large companies develop or acquire the necessary product lines to become preferred providers (i.e., gain a spot on a short list of supplier companies that managed plans go to for their prescription drugs). Because of their financial strength and market clout, these pharmaceutical companies believe that they will be able to acquire almost any innovative new products they do not discover or develop in-house. While their drug discovery and development programs will benefit from access to abundant cash resources and an increase in critical mass, their business model is driven primarily by the clout of market capitalization.

Some midsize companies (e.g., Abbott, Eli Lilly, and GlaxoSmithKline) are restructuring to increase research productivity and operational efficiency. These companies are also looking to acquire smaller companies that can fill pipeline gaps, help them expand into new, more promising therapeutic areas, or strengthen their presence in emerging markets. These midsize companies typically focus on discovering and developing innovative new treatments but reserve the option to partner with other companies to help commercialize their products, particularly in markets or therapeutic categories where the partner has a strong presence. However, mid-size companies are not without their own challenges. Those with robust product pipelines will still be vulnerable to acquisition by larger companies. And despite their relatively modest organizational size, some of these companies may still need to strategically downsize their operations, thereby ridding themselves of obsolete or burdensome overhead and infrastructure. In doing so, most should be better able to avoid mistakes and poor decisions resulting from managing organizations that are too big.

Small companies (most biotechnology companies fall into this category) hope to exploit their intellectual property and expertise in a particular technology platform, product class, or therapeutic area. Their business model is simple: to discover one or more high-value therapeutic molecules (which they believe have significant market potential) that can either be sold or licensed to a larger company. Typically, these companies are highly focused on drug discovery and development and have no intention of commercializing their own products. These companies, however, are especially vulnerable to acquisition by larger companies. For investors who are looking for an exit strategy (a way to realize their return on investment), this is a positive thing, but destabilizing or dismantling a productive research organization is not in the best interest of a market that is looking for continued innovation.

Each of these strategies represents a rational approach to the evolving new healthcare market. The large, mega-merged company relies on critical mass and market presence, but those advantages may be offset by the organizational challenges discussed earlier in this book. Also, while these companies are busy with the distractions of integration (which may take decades), the evolving new healthcare market will be redefining itself and setting new expectations. Since large organizations are, by their very nature, slow to adapt to change, they may not have the organizational flexibility to make additional adjustments and restructurings on the fly as they merge while the market evolves. Some expertise will be acquired in a merger, but the evolving new healthcare market will make the overwhelming majority of personnel redundant, obsolete, or unnecessary. As a result, these companies will continue to be organizationally inefficient.

This author believes that most mega-mergers are short-term financial fixes for the mediocre performance of one or both organizations being merged. As a result, mega-companies are unlikely to accomplish the organizational and operational goals touted by the proponents of the merger. These deals are often encouraged by financial institutions and investment banking attorneys who specialize in mergers and acquisitions and who stand to reap huge financial rewards when the deal is completed. In addition, corporate officers, especially C-level executives, will likely walk away with millions of dollars in merger bonuses (on both sides), retention packages, and "golden handshakes" directly related to the successful completion of these mergers. The bottom line is that most mega-merger deals are driven more by personal financial gain than by an interest in creating shareholder value or increasing the likelihood of finding innovative new drugs.

One exception to the large company model is the continued growth of large generic drug companies (e.g., Teva, Watson, Mylan) that will market their products at even lower prices. While the complexities of these organizations still need to be appropriately managed, these companies are a perfect business fit for the evolving new healthcare market because they are designed to thrive on high volume and low profit margins. These companies also have the expertise and experience of running lean efficient operations and negotiating with government agencies, managed care plans, and the drug distribution system (wholesalers and drug-store chains). Competition for these large generic companies will come mostly from larger pharmaceutical companies with broad generic product lines (e.g., Novartis).

The evolving new healthcare market will also be a good fit for smaller research-driven companies. These companies are more likely to have a narrower but deeper research focus (think highly specialized diseases) and are better able to adapt to changing market dynamics and customer needs. They typically maintain a high standard of expertise and competence throughout the organization, and company growth is managed in a manner that is consistent with the level of organizational expertise available. Managerial oversight also tends to play a larger role in smaller companies, resulting in better performance management and more operational efficiencies. Defining organizational expectations, ensuring strategic and operational alignment, and maintaining communication are also easier in smaller companies. As is the case for any small company, the single biggest challenge will be access to cash, with most depending on licensing revenues and research milestone payments to provide consistent cash flow and sufficient profit margins to remain financially sound and to allow for continued investment in R&D.

Regardless of which organizational strategy a company decides to pursue, success in the evolving new healthcare market will require adherence to some fundamental tenets. First, the market, healthcare providers, patients, and investors alike want companies to deliver innovative products which are demonstrably better than currently available treatments. Second, they want and need lower prices for branded prescription products. And while these are not unreasonable demands, for most companies—especially large and mid-sized companies—they will require major changes to business models. Third, in order to regain the public's trust and increase both operational efficiency and R&D productivity, the following changes will need to be made:

1. Leadership
    a. Companies must reestablish a commitment to integrity. Integrity must become an explicit corporate expectation that is supported by uncompromised compliance and leadership by example. In the evolving new healthcare market, there can be no room for individual or corporate breaches of integrity (e.g., not disclosing all facts, engaging in misleading advertising and promotion, downplaying safety issues).
    b. Leadership must possess expertise. Those in management will have little credibility if they set a high

standard for organizational expertise but do not possess it themselves.

c. Companies need to get serious about organizational development (specifically management development). They need to intensify their training and focus on developing industry expertise, general management training, and leadership skills.

d. Organizational goals and objectives should drive performance and results. Diligent management oversight should assure organizational alignment, compliance with organizational expectations, and accountability.

e. Management must create a work environment that encourages open communication and guards against group-think and organizational inertia that exacerbate mistakes and poor decisions.

f. Corporate officers and managers must be held personally accountable (e.g., forfeit financial gains and lose their jobs) for unethical or illegal activities that they should have been aware of and could have stopped.

2. Research and development
   a. Companies must focus on fewer therapeutic areas with broader and deeper comprehension of the diseases being studied.
   b. Companies must recruit, hire, and maintain world-class teams of researchers with expertise in the therapeutic areas of interest.
   c. Research goals and objectives must include a comprehensive understanding (broader and deeper) of diseases that will ultimately lead to prevention or cure, rather than just finding another active compound.
   d. Companies must eliminate development projects that do not have the potential to generate preventive treatments or cures or that are unlikely to demonstrate clinical superiority over currently available treatments.
   e. Research capabilities will need to include diagnostic expertise to develop the tools necessary in an era of personalized medicine.
   f. Companies must increase their commitment to scientific communications (e.g., presentations, publications, and data disclosures in press releases and investor relations discussions), and they must be complete, accurate, and

truthful and must disclose any potential or perceived conflicts of interest.

3. Marketing and sales
   a. Marketers must stop using commercialization tactics (traditional or otherwise) that mislead the market and put patients at risk *by emphasizing benefits and downplaying safety issues in an effort to drive sales*
   b. *Off-label promotion is illegal and must stop.*
   c. Companies must discontinue any tactics intended to inappropriately influence prescribing by providing direct or indirect financial or other benefits to healthcare providers.
   d. Marketers must build teams of expertise in managed markets (e.g., understand how to navigate complex payer systems, be skilled in pricing negotiations, and know how to educate providers within a restricted healthcare environment).
   e. Marketers must abandon the stereotypical detail-person model and their traditional sales tactics.
   f. Marketers must replace sales organizations with smaller medical specialty groups of individuals with life-science degrees and medical expertise in specific diseases or therapeutic areas.
   g. Pricing based on what the market will bear must end. Pricing strategies must reflect value that is supported by clinically relevant and meaningful proof of cost benefit.
   h. Per product price increases (not the average of the product line) should not exceed the annual increase in the Consumer Price Index.
4. Reductions in operating infrastructure and expenses
   a. Budgeting should be zero-based (start from nothing) and driven only by what is absolutely necessary (e.g., regulatory and legal requirements, customer-driven support, or efficiency-based investments). Past budgets are meaningless and do not justify operating budget proposals going forward.
   b. Companies must eliminate waste and any expenses that might be perceived as extravagant (e.g., the number of corporate jets and other aircraft, executive dining, limousine services, etc.).

c. Companies must eliminate facilities, people, and support systems that no longer have a role in the evolving new healthcare market.
d. Companies must reduce the fixed-cost base and should outsource whatever is not a core competency (e.g., information technology, routine laboratory testing, clinical trial execution, and marketing communications).

Some companies may feel that they are already taking many of these actions. Most, however, are merely going through the motions at best. Others may feel that these actions are impractical or might place them at a competitive disadvantage to those companies not taking some of these important steps. The fact is these steps are critical for long-term profitability in the evolving new healthcare market. These steps will help rebuild public trust and confidence in the industry, enhance productivity and efficiency, and help maximize profits while providing more pricing flexibility. Most importantly, these actions will create an environment that can leverage good leadership, enhance the value of diligent management oversight, and exploit research expertise to deliver the innovative new products the market demands. In the long run, these steps will not only create competitive advantage but will provide continued profitability that can fuel ongoing costly research and increase the probability of success.

Chapter 16
The Pharmaceutical Industry of the Future

Throughout this book, I have tried to explain how the pharmaceutical industry has evolved to its present state and what it needs to do going forward. The industry remains an $825 billion global business that will continue to grow, albeit at a slower rate than in the past. Nevertheless, companies that recognize the tremendous need for change and begin to strategically align themselves with the evolving new healthcare market can create a sustainable competitive advantage and still generate robust revenues and healthy profits.

For those industry executives who have been asleep at the switch these past few years, let me reiterate five realities about the evolving new healthcare market:

1. Delivery of healthcare will be increasingly managed;
2. Pricing pressures will increase as the managed market looks for ways to reduce and control costs;
3. The industry cannot remain profitable and retain its large, expensive infrastructures and inefficient operations.
4. Traditional industry marketing and sales tactics will become ineffective and obsolete;
5. Proprietary branded products will have to meet market expectations for superiority over currently available therapeutic options, and companies will have to provide the pharmacoeconomic data to support premium prices.

Near-term, depleted pipelines, patent expirations, and the arrival of more generic drugs in the marketplace will take their toll on revenue growth. At the same time, an aging population and healthcare reform will likely lead to increased use of prescription drugs as well as a renewed interest in disease prevention and programs to encourage patient compliance with drug therapy. In addition, companies that market products that are clinically proven to be the best treatment option available, that significantly improve health, or that disproportionately reduce other healthcare costs will receive unencumbered formulary approval and will be rewarded with premium prices. Healthcare plans will also encourage the use of these best in class products. Pharmaceutical research will strive for cures, clinically meaningful differentiation, and complementary diagnostic tests to accompany drug therapies. Easy-to-use in-office tests will help physicians make a definitive and rapid diagnosis, help identify patients who are most likely to respond to a particular treatment, and avoid prescribing products to those patients most likely to experience side effects.

Companies with differentiated products and a more market-focused business model supported by a corporate culture that values expertise, competence, and integrity will slowly regain market credibility and help transform an industry considered by many to be greedy and self-serving into one that finally puts patients ahead of profits. In short, companies that are aligned with the new market rather than at odds with it will have a higher probability of success.

So what will the industry look like in 2020 or 2030? There will be three pharmaceutical company models in the future: mega-companies, mid-sized companies, and very small companies. The few mega-companies will have large generic drug businesses, including biogeneric or biosimilar large molecule drugs (e.g., human growth hormone, erythropoietin, and filgrastim) that complement their broad proprietary branded product portfolios. These companies will combine market strength, from retooled commercialization infrastructures, with distribution channel (drug wholesalers and chain drugstores) management clout and the expertise to navigate the bureaucratic labyrinths of the evolving new market. Their product portfolios will be built more through acquisitions and partnering than on discovery research; their R&D will focus primarily on late-stage clinical development and regulatory approval of acquired products. The breadth of their product lines, the depth of their expertise, and their ability to invest in capital-intense infrastructure will make manufacturing, including contract manufacturing for smaller companies, a profit center and an important component of their core competencies. Smaller companies will look to these mega-companies for late-stage clinical development, assistance with regulatory submissions, and help with commercializing their newly discovered drugs.

In the future, more pharmaceutical companies will be mid-sized, targeting a few well-defined diseases or therapeutic areas. Steeped in world-class expertise and bolstered by collaborations with academic scientists throughout the world, their research teams will delve into the pathophysiology of diseases at the molecular level. Their comprehensive multidisciplinary approach to disease treatment will lend itself to complementary diagnostic test development. Complex molecules will be discovered or designed to interact with single or even multiple biologic targets, activating therapeutic responses while down-regulating (turning off) untoward physiologic responses that trigger side effects. The development of high-value treatments that fill significant unmet medical needs, prevent disease, or offer cures will eventually vindicate an industry that has held out these promises for decades, often with disappointing results.

Financial viability and profitability for these mid-sized and smaller companies will be driven by high-value innovative new products, lower operating expenses resulting from modest infrastructure investments, strategic use of outsourcing, and diligent expense management. Their resources will be concentrated on discovering and delivering mid-stage (Phase II or later) clinical trial candidates that have high value and a high probability of success. These companies will either partner with much larger companies for late-stage clinical trials or divest themselves of their drug candidates, especially if they are in therapeutic categories where a partner has a stronger commercialization presence. The smallest pharmaceutical companies will focus on drug discovery and bringing compounds to early-stage clinical proof-of-concept Phase II trials. These companies will have limited (i.e., laboratory-scale at most) if any manufacturing capabilities. Their commercial infrastructure will consist of a few highly skilled marketing specialists with expertise in commercial assessment of research portfolios, strategic product development, and business development licensing.

Perhaps one of the biggest changes that will result from the ongoing transformation of the industry is the volume of data and drug development information that will be available to the public. In an effort to provide transparency, enhance credibility, and mitigate the ongoing liability associated with non-disclosure, companies will begin posting virtually every piece of data they develop on the Internet. Storing and organizing all of this information electronically will be challenging, and the ongoing analysis, interpretation, and application of these massive amounts of data will require new systems, processes, and expertise. Imagine having every case report form for every clinical trial patient ever studied available on-line. As expected, medical and scientific publications as well as continuing medical education and conference presentations will become increasingly important vehicles for summarizing the original data and disseminating the analyses and conclusions derived from the clinical trial results.

Today, most pharmaceutical companies are too large to be managed effectively and efficiently in the new evolving healthcare market. Talent dilution and unmanageable size will continue to hamper those companies that are unwilling to take the necessary steps to manage the inherent complexities that afflict these large organizations. In addition to wasteful spending and diminished research productivity, these companies risk continued vulnerability from unchecked mistakes and poor decisions, negative publicity, diminished market credibility, and costly litigation. Reducing the expense burden of large, obsolete, and inefficient infrastructure will be critical to securing profitability in this challenging cost-conscious market.

Companies that succeed at delivering truly innovative treatments and reestablishing market credibility will have an opportunity to participate in a new market that promises to be as financially rewarding as any in the history of the industry. Smaller, simplified organizational structures with more narrowly defined market-sensitive business models will make managing these companies easier, with less risk and a higher probability for sustained profitability. The potential to prevent or cure diseases and reduce the need for other healthcare services through the use of complementary diagnostic testing will drive healthcare providers to encourage the use of innovative treatments and support premium, value-based pricing. Indeed, companies that can transform themselves, reestablish market credibility, deliver innovative products, and significantly reduce operating expenses stand to profit disproportionately with long-term financial viability that may be even greater in this new evolving market than could have been realized within the industry's current business model.

Imagine a future in which pharmaceutical companies with world-class research teams are finding the remarkable new treatment options that have been promised for decades and advancing the science of healthcare at a pace never before seen in the history of medicine. A future when years of competent leadership, a corporate commitment to integrity, and responsible commercialization tactics have reestablished the public's trust in the industry and made it a credible and trusted source of scientific and medical information. Imagine a future in which a focus on core competencies and strategic outsourcing provides healthy profits that are viewed by the market as necessary and deserved.

Continuing with this train of thought, imagine a future in which the industry finally puts patients ahead of everything else. A future in which generous philanthropy makes treatments affordable and available to all those in need, regardless of their ability to pay or where they live. A future in which the healthcare market is better informed of treatment options and their relative cost benefits. A future in which investors appreciate and understand the inherent challenges of the pharmaceutical industry but value its ability to bring innovative new products to the market and are willing to accept the vagaries of short-term financial performance because of potentially superior long-term returns on their investments.

Is all of this possible, or is it just so much wishful thinking? This author believes that competent leadership with the courage to make the necessary changes can make this vision a reality. Yes, venturing into new, unexplored territory involves risk and fear of the unknown. Will the changes work? How long will they take? What if they don't lead to the expected results? How will these changes affect profit and loss statements? Will investors understand what we are doing and, more importantly, will they continue to invest? Can management overcome its fear of personal financial loss that may result from these massive changes—concerns about bonuses and retirement and potential loss of face in an industry that values stability and predictability above all else and is often more concerned about who is up and who is down in the executive suite than about anything else. And last but not least, does the public understand that the lifeblood of the generic drug business is the continued development of innovative new drugs? Without them, there can be no new cheap generics.

The dramatic changes advocated throughout this book are a break from the traditional business model; they are untested and fraught with uncertainty. But in the final analysis, the likelihood that a company will succeed in the evolving new healthcare market depends on the competence and courage of its leadership team, the expertise and integrity of its employees, the quality and productivity of its research, the ability of management to act as agents of change and provide effective oversight, and the credibility of its scientific and corporate communications. Companies that embrace these changes will be well positioned in the 21st century to live up to the standard set by George W. Merck over sixty years ago when he said that "Medicine is for the people. It is not for the profits." Let's hope that today's pharmaceutical industry leaders finally see the light, have the foresight and courage to make the necessary changes, and begin to embrace his philosophy.

References

Chapter 1

1. IMS Health Press Release, October 7, 2009. www.imshealth.com
2. IMS Health Press Release, April 1, 2010. www.imshealth.com
3. National Center for Health Statistics, Life Expectancy at Birth, 65 and 85 years of age, U.S., Selected Years 1900-2006. www.cdc.gov/nchs
4. Commercial Insight: Antihypertensives: new fixed dose combinations unable to stem the tide of patent expirations. Datamonitor Report, July 28, 2009. www.datamonitor.com
5. The 200 best-selling prescription medicine: Table: sales 2008 rank. MedAd News. www.pharmalive.com

Chapter 2

1. Significant dates in U.S. food and drug law history. www.fda.gov
2. Changing the face of medicine, Dr. Frances Kathleen Oldham Kelsey. National Library of Medicine. www.nlm.nih.gov
3. Hughes B. 2009 FDA drug approvals. Nat Rev Drug Discov 2010;9:89-92.
4. Shalo S. The lifecycle of cipro, August 1, 2004. www.pharmexec.com.
5. Mossinghoff GJ. Overview of the Hatch-Waxman Act and its impact on the drug development process. Food Drug Law J 1999;54:187-194.
6. Jaeger K. GPhA marks the 25th anniversary of the Hatch-Waxman Act today. Press Release, September 24, 2009. Generic Pharmaceutical Association. www.gphaonline.org
7. Generic drug sales continue to climb. Posted February 10, 2010. www.icis.com
8. Financial statements for Teva Pharmaceutical-SP ADR (Teva). www.investing.businessweek.com.

9. Brown J. Special feature: global marketing. MedAd News, August 2001. Data referenced from IMS Health.
10. Molinder HK. The development of cimetidine: 1964-1976. A human story. J Clin Gastroenterol 1994;19(3):248-254.
11. Centers for Medicare and Medicaid Services. Historical National Health Expenditures: Table 2, Calendar Years 1960-2008. www.cms.hhs.gov/NationalHealthExpendData/downloads/tables.pdf
12. Spellberg B, Powers J, Brass E, et al. Trends in antimicrobial drug development: implications for the future. Clin Infect Dis 2004; 38:1279–1286.
13. Update: Influenza Activity—United States, 2001-2002 Season. MMWR Weekly 2002;51(49):1127.

Chapter 3

1. PhRMA 2009 Profile Key Facts. www.phrma.org
2. MedAd News, September 2009, p 12.
3. Research for people report. Posted on NIH website. www.nih.gov/about/budget.htm
4. IMS Health, MIDAS, Market Segmentation Feature, MAT, September 2008, as reported in Generic Pharmaceutical Association 2009 Annual Report, p 30. www.gphaonline.org
5. IMS Health Press Release, October 7, 2009. www.imshealth.com
6. PhRMA 2009 Profile, Table 8, p 56. www.phrma.org
7. IMS Health Press Release, April 1, 2010. www.imshealth.com
8. Goldberg R. Big pharma shoves America off the wagon, July 9, 2009. Data referenced in Advertising Age. www.minyanville.com
9. Data from SDI, Yardley, Pennsylvania (see Figure 9-1).
10. Dept. of Justice Press Release, October 3, 2001. www.justice.gov/opa/pr/2001/October/513civ.htm
11. Press Release: Lupron Settlement, December 1, 2004. www.hagens-berman.com
12. Armstrong D, Wilde Matthews A. Pfizer case signals tougher action on off-label drug use. Wall Street Journal, May 14, 2004.
13. Dept. of Justice Press Release, May 13, 2004. www.justice.gov/opa/pr/2004/May/04_civ_322.htm

14. Dept. of Justice Press Release, September 2, 2009. www.fbi.gov/pressrel/pressrel09/justice_090209.htm
15. United States District Court, District of Massachusetts, Criminal Number: 09 CR 10258-DPW, October 9, 2009.
16. AstraZeneca to pay $520 million for off-label drug marketing. Dept. of Justice Press Release, April 27, 2010. www.justice.gov
17. Novartis Vaccines & Diagnostics to pay more than $72 million to resolve False Claims Act allegations concerning TOBI. Dept. of Justice Press Release, May 4, 2010. www.justice.gov
18. Weintraub M. Long-term weight control: The National Heart, Lung, and Blood Institute funded multimodal intervention study. Clin Pharmacol Therap 1992;51:581-646.
19. Lemonick D, Dowell W, Nash M, et al. The new miracle drug? *TIME*, September 23, 1996.
20. Levine S. *The Redux Revolution*. New York: William Morrow and Co., 1996.
21. www.fundinguniverse.com/company-histories/Wyeth-Company-History.html
22. Testimony by Ann Marie Cisneros before the House Energy and Commerce Committee Subcommittee on Oversight and Investigations, February 13, 2007. www.archives.energycommerce.house.gov
23. Letter to Andrew C. von Eschenbach, MD, December 19, 2007. www.finance.senate.gov/press/Gpress/2007/prg122007a.pdf
24. U.S. Dept. of Justice, Drug Enforcement Administration, Office of Diversion Control Summary of Medical Examiner Reports on Oxycodone-Related Deaths www.deadiversion.usdoj.gov/drugs_concern/oxycodone/oxycontin7.htm
25. The United States Attorney's Office, Western District of Virginia Press Release, May 10, 2007. www.dodig.mil/IGInformation/IGInformationReleases/purdue_frederick_1.pdf
26. Kaiser Public Opinion Spotlight, April 2008. www.kff.org/spotlight/rxdrugs/upload/Rx_Drugs.pdf

Chapter 7

1. Medicine: what the doctor ordered. *TIME*, August 18, 1952. www.time.com

Chapter 8

1. Filmore D. It's a GPCR world. Modern Drug Discovery November 2004, pp 24-28.

Chapter 9

1. Saul S. Gimme an Rx! Cheerleaders pep up drug sales. NY Times, November 28, 2005. www.nytimes.com/2005/11/28/business/28cheer.html
2. PhRMA adopts new marketing code. PhRMA Press Release, April 19, 2002. www.phrma.org/news_room/press_releases
3. SafeRx Amendment Act of 2008, the Council of the District of Columbia, Codification District of Columbia Official Code, 2001 Edition. www.dccouncil.washington.dc.us/images

Chapter 10

1. DTC spending stabilized in 2009 amid strong growth for cable, Internet adspend. Medical Marketing & Media. www.mmm-online.com
2. Weintraub A. Ask your doctor if this ad is right for you. BusinessWeek, November 4, 2009, Source data from market researcher Verilogue Inc.
3. Report to Congressional Requesters: United States Government Accountability Office (GAO), November 2006: Prescription drugs: improvements needed in FDA's oversight of direct-to-consumer advertising: GAO-07-54. www.gao.gov/new.items/d0754.pdf
4. Law M, Soumerai S, Adams A, Mjumdar S. Costs and consequences of direct-to-consumer advertising for clopidogrel in Medicaid. Arch Intern Med 2009;169:1969-1974.
5. Promotional spending for prescription drugs. Congressional Budget Office, December 2, 2009. www.cbo.gov/ftpdocs
6. Schondelmeyer SW. Insight on the issues, Rx watchdog re-port: drug prices continue to climb despite lack of growth in general inflation rate. AARP Public Policy Institute, November 2009.
7. Warner-Lambert to pay $430 million to resolve criminal and civil health care liability relating to off-label promotion. Dept. of Justice Press Release, May 13, 2004. www.justice.gov
8. Elliott C. The drug pushers. Atlantic Magazine, April 2006.

9. Kowalczyk L. 60 doctors took speaker fees from drug giant. The Boston Globe, September 29, 2009. www.boston.com
10. Testimony of Steven Nissen, MD, Chairman, Dept. of Cardiovascular Medicine, The Cleveland Clinic, to the Senate Aging Committee: Hearing on Education and Research: higher learning or higher earning? July 29, 2009 (comment made during Q&A viewable on video of testimony). www.aging.senate.gov
11. Testimony of Murray Kopelow, MD, MS (Comm.), FRCPC, Chief Executive, Accreditation Council for Continuing Medical Education (ACCME), to the Senate Aging Committee: Hearing on Education and Research: higher learning or higher earning? July 29, 2009. www.aging.senate.gov
12. GSK limits medical education funding to independent programs with highest impact on patient care, GSK Press Release, September 21, 2009.
13. Pfizer changes its funding of Continuing Medical Education in the U.S., Press Release, July 2, 2008.
14. Richter R. Stanford adopts new approach to continuing medical education to prevent industry influence. Stanford University website, January 11, 2010. www.ed.stanford.edu

Chapter 11

1. Speech before PhRMA Annual Meeting, April 3, 2004, Remarks by Lester M. Crawford, DVM, PhD, Acting Commissioner of the FDA. www.fda.gov
2. PhRMA 2007 Profile, p 5. www.phrma.org
3. Gutierrez C. Market Scan, Pfizer washes its hands of Exubera, October 18, 2007. www.forbes.com
4. Bombardier C, Laine L, Reicin A, et al. Comparison of upper gastrointestinal toxicity of rofecoxib and naproxen in patients with rheumatoid arthritis. N Engl J Med 2000;343:1520-1528.
5. Merck announces voluntary worldwide withdrawal of Vioxx®, Press Release, September 30, 2004. www.merck.com
6. Merck halts Vioxx sales. Posted September 30, 2004. Updated October 5, 2004 by Rita Rubin. www.usatoday.com
7. Mukherjee D, Nissen SE, Topol EJ. Risk of cardiovascular events associated with selective COX-2 inhibitors. JAMA 2001; 286:954-959.
8. Editorial. Vioxx: an unequal partnership between safety and efficacy. Lancet 2004;364:1287-1288.

9. Merck announces voluntary worldwide withdrawal of Vioxx®, Press Release, September 30, 2004.
10. Waxman HA. The lessons of Vioxx-drug safety and sales. N Engl J Med 2005;352:2576-2578.
11. Agreement to resolve U.S. Vioxx® product liability lawsuits, Merck Press Release, November 9, 2007.

Chapter 12

1. Letter From PhRMA President and CEO. PhRMA 2009 Profile www.phrma.org
2. Harvard Business School. The awards of alumni achievement, 2002. www.hbs.edu
3. www.Pfizer.com
4. Headliner: Novartis' Joseph Jimenez. Medical Marketing & Media, May 2008.

Chapter 13

1. Prescription Drug User Fee Act (PDUFA), FDA and Stakeholders Public Meeting, Comments of National Consumers League. Brett Kay, Health Policy Associate, September 15, 2000, Washington, DC. www.fda.gov
2. Reauthorizing the prescription drug user fee act: how are PDUFA, the FDA budget, and drug safety related? George Washington School of Public Health and Health Services, April 2007. www.gwumc.edu
3. Richter R. School restricts industry funding of CME courses. Stanford School of Medicine report. September 10, 2008. www.med.stanford.edu/mcr/2008/cme-0910.html
4. Richter R. Stanford adopts new approach to continuing medical education to prevent industry influence. Stanford University website post, January 11, 2010. www.med.stanford.edu
5. Testimony of Murray Kopelow, MD, MS (Comm.), FRCPC, Chief Executive, Accreditation Council for Continuing Medical Education (ACCME), to the Senate Aging Committee: Hearing on Education and Research: higher learning or higher earning? July 29, 2009. www.aging.senate.gov
6. Schondelmeyer SW. Insight on the issues, Rx watchdog report: drug prices continue to climb despite lack of growth in general inflation rate. AARP Public Policy Institute, November 2009.

7. Jaeger K. GPhA marks the 25th anniversary of the Hatch-Waxman Act today. Press Release, September 24, 2009. Generic Pharmaceutical Association. www.gphaonline.org

Chapter 14

1. Drug makers agree to offer Medicare discounts. NY Times (Reuters), June 21, 2009. www.nytimes.com
2. CMS national health expenditures by type of service and source of funds, CY 1960-2008. www.cms.gov
3. CMS national health expenditure projections 2008-2018, Forecast summary. www.cms.hhs.gov
4. Written Statement to Senate Special Committee on Aging, Mark Pearson, Head, Health Division, OECD, September 30, 2009. Disparities in health expenditure across OECD countries: Why does the United States spend so much more than other countries? www.oecdwash.org
5. Danzon PM, Furukawa MF. Prices and availability of pharmaceuticals: evidence from nine countries. Health Affairs Web Exclusive. Project HOPE—The People-to-People Health Foundation, Inc., October 29, 2003. www.content.healthaffairs.org
6. Remarks by Margaret Hamburg, MD, Commissioner of Food and Drugs, on Effective Enforcement and Benefits to Public Health. Food and Drug Law Institute video webinar, August 6, 2009. www.fda.gov

Index

A

B

C

Q

R

S

T

U

V

W

Z